Rocks and Feathers

A memoir by Maureen Lane

The kookaburra is Maureen Lane's totem, given to her by a South Australian Aboriginal Elder at a peace and justice event held at University of Melbourne.

Publisher information

Rocks and Feathers: A Memoir by Maureen Lane
is published by Stories to Keep.

First published in Australia 2024 by Stories to Keep Pty Ltd.

ABN 19362876762

Storiestokeep.com.au

Words copyright: Maureen Lane ©.

This work is in copyright. Apart from any use as permitted under the Copyright Act 1968, no part may be reproduced, copied, scanned stored in a retrieval system, recorded or transmitted in any form or by any means without the publisher's prior written permission.

Stories to Keep

PO Box 5012

Brunswick Vic 3056.

National Library of Australia Cataloguing-in-Publication data:

Author: Maureen Lane

Title: Rocks and Feathers: A Memoir by Maureen Lane.

ISBN: 978-0-6452457-3-8

Subjects: Maureen Lane, 1951-; Footscray-Yarraville-Altona mid-century history; cinema history; Beatles; Australian music; Teaching; workplace injury. Autobiography: Maureen Lane.

Cover and book Design: Christina Carter.

Typeset in Times New Roman, 10pt

Printed and bound at Ingram Spark/Lightning Source, 76 Discovery Road, Dandenong South, Vic Australia 3175.

Stories to Keep acknowledges the traditional custodians of country in which this Australian story takes place. We pay our respects to First Nations elders past and present and extend that respect to all Aboriginal and Torres Strait Islander Peoples.

About the author

Maureen Lane is the third child of Gerry and Linda Lane, the mother of two daughters, wife to David, a teacher, published author, historian, community activist, artist and member of the Society of Women Writers Victoria. Maureen has a deep connection to people and has committed to paper the stories of many other people. Maureen believes that when someone shares their personal story, they reach out and connect with the reader. The reader is invited into the author's world being transported into an era, culture, event, to share philosophy and feelings. This is her sixth book and her first memoir.

Other books by Maureen Lane

Pubs, Punts and Pastures: The Story of Irish Pioneer Women on the Salt Water River with Joan Carstairs. Published by St Albans History Society.

Altona & Surrounds: A Patchwork of Memories. Published by Altona-Laverton Historical Society Incorporated in 2018.

A Bush Hospital By The Bay: Altona Hospital 1932 to 1996 with Ann Cassar, Jim Hevey and Graeme Reilly. Published by Altona-Laverton Historical Society Incorporated in 2018.

Putting the Fun Back into Drag Racing. Published by Australian Nostalgia Racers Victoria Incorporated in 2020.

Angels with David King. Published by Melbourne Books in 2021.

Introduction

It was a chance comment from a young First Nations woman, but, like the ripple from a stone in a pond, it would resonate, and continues to do so. The young woman was telling me about Diamond Creek's local history as we stood on the street. Unexpectedly, a tear welled in her eye. Just moments earlier, a random stranger had directed a racist slur at her. Embarrassed, I apologised for the stranger's abhorrent language.

I can still hear the heaviness in her voice when she responded to me:

"We all carry an invisible backpack. In it are the stories of our ancestors and our own story of injustices." She confided her truth about the injustices that she continually faced and the weight she bore.

Her words have stayed with me, and I have mulled them over in my mind, shaping them and accommodating them into a part of my own personal philosophy.

The conclusion I have come to is that all our life experiences – the injustices, the achievements, the good times and bad, the things we do and say, and how we relate to each other – make us who we are. We carry all our history in our personal backpacks: the heavy rocks of negativity and the lightness of feathers that symbolise the positives in life.

These good and bad experiences we carry affect the way we go forward – stooped or tall. The lightness or heaviness of our footfall depends on what we carry with us. The weight of our historic backpacks, the paths we follow and the ways we tackle obstacles in that path shape the person we become.

That Aboriginal woman was strong and proud despite, or because of, the wounds inflicted by a racist comment. She would carry that comment because it hurt. Another stone to carry in her backpack.

Pondering my life journey, I wondered how I became who I am today. I concluded that I am that person because of strangers I have met, places I have been, books I have read and films I have seen and because of family and friends who continue to nurture me.

I was an incredibly lucky child, born to loving, hard-working, kind and welcoming parents. I am the youngest of three, raised by the whole family. I learnt from them what love can be.

While I searched for the rare kind of love my parents shared, my turbulent teens brought with them many mistakes and learning curves.

At times, the road was rough and I felt lost, but through the love and support of family and a few good friends, I found my destiny in my children, my work and the unlikely love of my life, David.

David opened my eyes to the difficulties faced by other families in the 1950s and '60s and made me appreciate my childhood circumstances. David has a whole lot of different weights in his backpack, which he shares with me, while I share mine with him, making them lighter.

My backpack is still heavy at times, but now it holds more feathers than rocks and I am stronger because of its contents.

Through these pages, I share my life of "rocks and feathers" with you. I hope my story will help you carry your load and walk a little lighter on your way.

CHAPTER 1
The Beginning

"Get away with you, Gerry," Mum giggled like a schoolgirl.

She was bent over the kitchen sink and elbow-deep in dirty dishwater when Dad slipped his arms around her waist, squeezed her tightly and kissed her neck. She spun around and pushed him away, leaving a wet handprint on his shirt and a smile on her face. Their lips met for a quick peck and she was back to the dishes.

Dad was always smooching up to Mum, on holiday or at home.

That frequent scene summed up my parents' relationship. Gerry Lane, Dad, the exuberant lover, adored Mum and was never shy of showing the world his feelings. Mum, Linda Mullins, was only 16 when she met Gerry at a "susso" dance in Footscray in 1934. Susso was short for sustenance – a term given to the payments received from the government to men who wanted to work but were unable to find employment during the Great Depression (the time between the two world wars). For many families in Melbourne's west, the susso was the only thing between them and starvation. In the true Aussie tradition of helping out a mate, susso dances sprang up around the state. The price of admission into one of these dances was an item of food to be distributed to those who needed it most.

Gerry was 19 when he met Linda. They danced together at the susso dance, and then Gerry moved on to ask another girl to dance, while his mate asked Linda to do him the honour.

"Gerry's a really good dancer. I could dance with him all night," Linda shouted over the music while she danced with his mate.

The friend dutifully relayed the message. Linda and Gerry danced all night and through the next 55 years of marriage.

Linda

Linda was a shy girl – slim and pretty with hazel eyes and shoulder-length dark hair. She was from pioneer stock and quietly proud of her heritage.

Whenever Linda passed Footscray Gardens, she would wistfully lament: "All that land used to belong to our family, but we were swindled out of it."

She had grown up on stories of Aboriginal King Billy and his family camping on the river near the gardens each night. Soldiers would round up any Aboriginal people in the Melbourne area at dusk and throw them in jail or worse. Each night some people from the Wurundjeri clan of the Kulin Nation camped on the banks of the Saltwater River, now known as the Maribyrnong River – a word in the traditional owners' tongue meaning "I can hear a ring-tailed possum." Of course, the land belonged to the Aboriginal people, who had a different understanding of ownership. They considered the land their responsibility and were our original conservationists, moving from camp to camp so as to not fish out a stream, overharvest vegetation and ensure the continuation of species. This way of life also meant they had a varied diet.

King Billy – a community leader dubbed "King" by the government – and his family were neighbours to Linda's great grandma, Margaret (Dowd) Pickett. Margaret traded her flour, milk and sugar for their eels and fish. The Aboriginal boys welcomed her boys into their friendship group and taught them how to fish for their own eels.

Margaret Dowd had come from Ireland in 1839 and worked across the rickety wooden slab bar in a pub in Melbourne's Little Collins Street, before meeting and marrying William Pickett. They lived in a tent off Little Bourke Street in the early 1840s. Here their three children were born before the little family settled in Saltwater – as Footscray was known then. It was here, in The Ship Inn, that Margaret gave birth to Linda's grandmother, Elizabeth – the first white child born in the district. Linda was proud of her heritage and the fact that her ancestors had co-existed peacefully with the Aboriginal people and become friends at a time when Aboriginal lives did not matter.

Linda may have been proud of her mother's line, but she was not enamoured of her father. She was raised in a violent household. Her father was a slaughterman – hard-drinking, loud, rough and violent. He regularly beat Linda's mother, Kate, while Linda and her siblings hid under the kitchen table to avoid his fists. He also kept another woman, to Kate's shame and her family's financial cost.

Mum (middle) with Auntie Dorrie (right) stepping out on the town.

Linda's father slaughtered cattle at Newmarket Yards near Footscray Park in the 1930s and '40s. Every Friday, Linda and older sister Dorrie had to take the afternoon off school to go to the gates of the slaughter yards. There they waited with other family members of slaughter yard workers. The girls took a wheelbarrow with them to carry home the offal given away to family members as a kind of bonus for the workers. Offal was tripe, liver, meat off-cuts and the occasional pig's trotter.

On one of these excursions, Dorrie and Linda were wheeling the empty barrow across Lynch's Bridge, Footscray, when a herd of frantic bulls broke loose and stampeded down the road. The two little girls were on the bridge when they saw the marauding, terrified beasts make their bid for freedom. The frightened girls abandoned the barrow and jumped off the bridge, rolling down the embankment to stop just short of the foul river water turned blood red by the runoff from the slaughter yard. The herd galloped by with yard workers in hot pursuit while the girls retrieved the wheelbarrow before continuing on their way to collect the week's rations.

Gerry's Heritage

Gerry came from a little farm called Crowlands, just outside the country town of Ararat, about 200km northwest of Footscray. The district of Crowlands is named after Gerry's family farm. His father, George Henry "Harry" Lane, was a gold miner and gravedigger, but, like all families in Crowlands, his grandparents had been farmers, too.

Gerry's farmer relatives bartered produce to vary their diets and share their harvest with friends and neighbours. When the orchard trees' branches groaned under the weight of ripe and juicy apricots, cherries, peaches, apples and nectarines, the fruit would be swapped for a side of beef, lamb or even some jars of sweet, golden honey from a cousin's hives.

This practice continued up until the 1960s when a new generation found jobs in the towns. With fewer workers and more cash, the farm's barter system weakened after being reliable for decades.

In Dad's words:

"The aunts at Crowlands used to make cakes; they weren't too good. We used to call them 'bullets.' Aunty Nora used to make soup in a big cauldron over the open fireplace in the kitchen. She would stir the soup with a cigarette hanging out of her mouth. We would be watching as the ash got longer and longer, waiting for it to fall. If it fell into the soup, Mary just stirred it into the soup. Us kids never liked to eat what she had cooked.

The old aunties bottled a lot of fruit on the farms and sometimes they kept it for a year in the bottle. They made their own wine, too. They used to press the grapes by hand with a press. One day, a rat got into the wine press and died and no one knew until they got the mast [skins and pip] out. Needless to say, they didn't drink the wine that year – they sold it.

There was an Indian hawker [travelling salesman] who used to come around on a horse and cart, and everyone would be anxious for him to come. He sold nuts, bolts, pots, pans – everything. The women would stretch out the bolts of cloth on the road.

The grocer used to call once a week and take the order, then deliver the following week. The same with the baker, but the families made most of their own bread. They all had cows to keep them going with butter, milk and cream.

My maiden aunts, Aunty Mary and Aunty Nora, lived together at Crowlands after my grandfather died, and they used to fight all the time. They even fought over who owned which chickens. When they fed them, the chooks settled the argument. Each hen ran to its owner. You wouldn't have believed that, would you?

We liked Nora and Mary. We had another aunty, Sarah, who lived at Ararat. She was my dad's sister, and we didn't like her that much. She wore a tea cosy on her head and pulled it right down to her eyes. She was dirty, and we never liked to eat anything she cooked. She was kind-hearted, though, and was always offering us food. We didn't like to take any, though."

Gerry loved his mother, Margaret (nee Griffin) Lane, and loved spending time with her. He described her as a real country girl – warm, loving and hardworking. She was part of an extended family in the area, and her cleanliness and cooking skills outshone those of the old aunties – something for which Gerry was very grateful.

In the early 1920s, when Gerry was in primary school, his family moved to 3 Beaumont Parade, West Footscray, but Crowlands remained his spiritual home. He would visit his old aunties there at least once a year and always looked after his parents' grave in the Ararat cemetery – meticulously removing weeds and replacing the white pebbles that topped the gravesite. He placed fresh flowers on top to show that the inhabitants were loved.

Gerry was a great storyteller, regaling Linda with stories about his father's gold mining adventures in Western Australia.

"My father was George Henry Lane, but everyone called him Harry. He and his brother, Joe, decided to go prospecting in Western Australia, and

they travelled overland through South Australia where they met up with an adventurous Aboriginal boy, Sugarbag, who wanted to go with them. They took him along to look after the pit ponies in the mines. Miners took small ponies down the main shaft, carrying equipment into the mines and carrying the rock and dirt out to be sorted in the daylight.

When they got to the goldfields in WA, they set up a tent to camp in together. Harry only owned two things of any value – a mouth organ and the silver pocket watch that his mother had given him for his 21st birthday.

After a long day of prospecting, Harry, Joe and Sugarbag returned to the campsite to find the tent trampled to the ground and Harry's mouth organ and his pocket watch gone. Harry was very upset about his watch. It had such sentimental value. His mother didn't have a lot of money, and it was a really beautiful thing inscribed, "To Harry Lane from his mother 1903." He loved that watch.

Sugarbag saw how upset Harry was and proclaimed, "I'll catch him for ya, Harry!" and he set about tracking the culprit. Harry and Joe followed Sugarbag until he suddenly crouched down behind some rocks. The two brothers did the same. Then they heard the mouth organ being blown and sucked, blown and sucked, making a terrible racket. A tall, thin Aboriginal man was perched on a bolder with the mouth organ between his lips and the watch in one hand. He shook the watch and held it to his ear to listen to the ticking; then he smashed it onto the rock over and over again.

Sugarbag jumped up and ran at the surprised native and they fought for a short while before the thief threw the mouth organ and watch on the ground and ran off. Sugarbag proudly walked back to Harry with the watch and mouth organ in his open hands, a huge smile on his face. Harry was so grateful to get his watch back that he gave the mouth organ to Sugarbag as a reward.

When the miners realised that they were not going to strike it rich, they returned home, via Sugarbag's country. They gave him a pit pony as payment, which was the cause of great excitement in his camp and gave Sugarbag new prestige in the tribe."

Linda and Gerry: The Courting Days

Linda and Gerry started courting almost immediately after meeting at the dance. At first, Gerry would call for Linda on a pushbike. She would sit on the crossbar so he could peddle. This was called having a dink on the bike and was a popular mode of transport during the 20th Century. Later, he bought an old motorcycle and used his skills as a self-taught mechanic to get it running. This created a whole new world of freedom. The couple could go for longer trips in relative comfort.

Linda perched on the back of the motorcycle with her basket full of sandwiches and a thermos flask of tea while they headed to Ararat to meet the rest of the Lane family. The pilgrimage back to Crowlands was to become a yearly excursion and a tradition they maintained all their lives. That tradition has now passed to me.

Gerry nervously asked Linda's father for her hand in marriage and then purchased a blue sapphire ring with tiny diamonds on each side of the setting. Of course, she said, "Yes." They were so much in love and stayed that way all their lives.

They married at St Monica's Catholic Church, Footscray, in 1936, in front of family and friends. As the smiling bride

Linda and Gerry courting.

walked down the aisle on her father's arm, she shuddered with embarrassment as his girlfriend greeted him. He had invited the "other woman" to his daughter's wedding – another indignity for Linda's mother, Kate, to suffer.

"It spoilt my day to see her sitting next to the aisle, bold as brass," Linda said. "No shame. Poor Mum. She was so embarrassed. I never forgave my father for doing that. He spoilt my wedding day."

The Family Way

The happy married couple had no money for a honeymoon but moved into a rented house at 50 Fehon Street in Yarraville. Guests were welcomed into the Lanes' home. Linda's cousin, Percy Mullins, and his fiancée, Joan, stayed with the newlyweds while their own home was being built. Percy slept on the lounge room floor while Joan slept on a bed in a built-in part of the back porch.

Linda would lay in bed and hear the ticking of Percy's watch as he tiptoed past the bedroom door in the middle of the night.

"Percy's going into Joan's room," she whispered through the darkness into Gerry's ear, "I can hear his watch ticking."

Gerry rolled over with a wry smile on his lips, "I always said you had good hearing."

Joan and Percy moved into their own home and Gerry's younger brother, Frank, started going with Pat Keenan. They had been courting for a short time when Frank moved into the verandah bedroom vacated by Joan. Pat used to come and stand outside the house and wait for Frank to come and take her out.

"It's a bit odd that Pat doesn't come in," said Linda, but she decided that it takes all kinds.

When Frank and Pat tied the knot, they moved into the Yarraville house while their home was being built.

When I was a toddler, my nan, Kate Mullins, moved into our house. Nan's husband had moved another woman into their home in Footscray and put Nan's meagre possessions on the front lawn. When she came back from her daily visit to her elderly mother, she was locked out.

It was a huge embarrassment for Nan, made worse by the local paper's page-one story that read, "Wife Out, Lady Friend In."

Initially, Nan had gone to live with my Aunty Dorrie, Uncle Dan Heffernan and their children Jack and Dorothy. Dorrie took a job working for a dentist, Dr Pedley, who lived in a double-storey house opposite the Yarraville post office. Dorrie cleaned the Pedleys' house and was a nanny to their children.

When Nan came to live at our house, our little family was complete.

Camping Cousins

A close bond between Gerry and Linda and Pat and Frank was formed after my aunt and uncle married. They began a tradition of holidaying together. Frank was Gerry's youngest brother and he always took care of him. The two men liked each other's company, so they decided to pack a tent and trailer to go camping. That was the only kind of holiday they could afford. Gerry, being a bit of a bushman, loved to get back to nature. He would point out edible sap on gum trees, where to find water in the bush and how to survive if they got lost. Gerry had a love of nature and shared his knowledge with Frank and, later, his children. The two couples packed up an old two-wheeled trailer with everything they would need for a few days sleeping in a tent and cooking over an open fire. Gerry always took a small-handled axe for firewood. A metal bucket and a shovel would come in handy to dig a toilet. Sometimes Joan and Percy went as well.

The women packed food, a washbowl, a billycan and Velvet soap that would be used with creek water to do the dishes as well as for washing clothes and bathing.

For the women, bathing involved carefully picking their way across the stones at the bottom of an icy creek, a few squeals as they edged slowly into the running water and then a quick dunk under the ripples before a hasty retreat to the tents to get dressed. Gerry, Percy and Frank, on the other hand, just chased each other into the water, splashing and jumping about and making a game of it.

They all slept in tents under the stars and enjoyed nature in all her beauty. But on Saturday night they would find a town and make their way to a pub for a counter meal in the Ladies' Lounge. Eating in a restaurant was a rare treat.

The boys would enjoy a few beers, but Gerry was not a big drinker and would change to a shandy – a mixture of half beer and half lemonade – as the night wore on. That was what the ladies liked to drink, too. Frank and Percy teased Gerry, but he didn't care. He knew his limits.

After one such camping holiday, Joan and Linda confided that there would be no more camping experiences for them. They were both pregnant.

Everyone was delighted when Linda announced to family and friends that she and Gerry were going to have a baby. The first thing they did was to go to Crowlands to tell Gerry's mother, Margaret, the good news. She longed for a grandchild and was ecstatic at the announcement. The new baby, if it was a girl, would be called Margaret after her.

It was a difficult confinement. Linda was very sick and lost weight. She suspected there might be something amiss, but the doctors dismissed her concerns as those of an overanxious first-time mother.

After carrying the baby to full term, Linda delivered little Margaret, but the joy was short-lived as the tiny baby survived only for a few minutes. The little lifeless body was whisked away without even being sighted by her mother. Linda was inconsolable. Gerry rocked her in his arms as their tears flowed.

The doctor warned the young couple not to have more children because Linda's health would not survive another pregnancy and confinement like the last. However, within a year Linda was expecting another baby.

Although they were delighted by the news, the shadow of little Margaret's birth and death hung over them. The doctor's words rang in their ears: she should not have any more children – "it was too dangerous for her health." Linda and Gerry pushed negative thoughts to the back of their minds and never spoke them out loud. As the due date came closer, Linda was confined to bed to rest until baby Gerald Junior made his way into the world – without incident. Unfortunately, his arrival was too late for our grandmother, Margaret. She passed away just before he was born.

Baby Barbara followed four years after Gerald, and I made my way into the world in 1951, seven years after her.

Maureen's baby tag, reads: Lane, Linda. Female. Weight: 6 lb 30oz. Length: 19½ inches. Time:1.10am. Date: 21.8.51.

Chubba bubba, me as a baby.

The youngest of the three children, I was mostly left to my own devices and found ways to entertain myself, much like an only child. My sister was past playing with toys. She helped Mum around the house a lot, especially with cooking. Barbara is an amazing cook and her sponges are to die for. She was more interested in going out with her friends, dancing and being part of teen groups, like the one that performed Gilbert and Sullivan operettas on stage at St Augustine's Church Hall, than playing with me. Barb sang in the chorus, danced, got to wear long dresses and attended the after-parties.

My brother, Gerald, suddenly became known as Gerry to his friends. He wanted a cooler name than the one the family used for him. When I was little, I called him "Woll-Woll." I couldn't pronounce Gerald. I still call him that sometimes.

Along with the new, cool name, "Gerry" wanted a leather jacket, but Mum wouldn't buy him one. She didn't want him looking like a hood and everyone saying, "There goes that boy in the leather jacket."

She bought him a green cardigan with a couple of white stripes on one arm, and he lived in that cardigan. We laughed when Gerald told us everyone was saying, "There goes that boy in the green cardigan."

Gerald had a really good singing voice and lots of personality. He was always the life and soul of any party, so it was only natural that he scored the main comic role in

Gilbert and Sullivan shows at St Augustine's. He played in *The Mikado, Trial by Jury* and was "the very model of a modern Major General" in *HMS Pinafore*. He went on to join other light opera companies and hung around with TV identities Pete Smith, Phillip Brady and Jim Murphy, who became a celebrated journalist, TV presenter and movie critic. Gerald went out with Jim's sister, Mary, for a while. All his friends became TV or radio celebrities in the 1960s. He still jokes, "I'm the only one I've never heard of."

My big brother was quite the ladies' man. When I was in prep grade at St Augustine's, he dated my prep teacher, Miss Fanning. He must have been a very good boyfriend because she spoiled me rotten.

Once, I asked Mum why I didn't have any brothers or sisters close to my age.

"We waited a long time to have you. I had to stay in the hospital for six weeks to bring you safely into the world," she said.

It wasn't until I was going through her meagre possessions after her funeral that I found a letter Dad had written to her in hospital on the day I was born. It explained how much I was wanted and loved.

"Hello Darling,
I thought I would write you a few lines just in case I cannot make it tomorrow. You know how things are at work so don't be disappointed if I am not in to see you. I told Gerald and Barbara about Maureen and they were very excited, more so Barbara. She said I would have to get busy and buy some clothes and a pram. Gerald said he would have liked a boy, but he admitted he was pleased inside. If Seales turns up tomorrow, I have a good chance of getting off, but if he doesn't I can't just leave them in the lurch, much as I want to see you and Maureen. Darling, you cannot imagine my feelings now that it is all over. It is just as if a weight has been lifted from my mind and nothing but happiness and freedom from worry remains. I have lived a lifetime since you have been away and every day was getting longer and longer wishing I could come in and see you. When I found out about Maureen, I did not get so very excited but instead, I had a terrible gnawing doubt that everything was not as good as it seems. I still remember our firstborn when they said that everything would be all right and I found out that you were very ill and we didn't have any baby. That is all past now darling and we can only look to many more years of happiness with our Gerald, Barbara and Maureen. We have three beautiful children now and that makes up for our unhappiness on the first occasion. I can tell you now my darling that I have relived those horrible memories over and over again, but now we are free from every worry and care. I know you have had a lot of lingering doubts these last six weeks, but neither of us was in a position to mention it until now. Well darling, I'll say goodnight to you and little Maureen until tomorrow night, I am yours forever,
Gerry XXX   X Maureen

Mum never got over losing that first child and would express her sadness about her loss even when she was in her 70s. Dad didn't say much. He would just put his head down and go quiet.

Gerry's letter to Linda when I was born.

CHAPTER 3
The Flood

On December 3, 1954, a disaster struck our home when the skies opened and torrential rains were dumped on Yarraville. The park next door turned into a raging river that flowed straight into our backyard, up the steps and into every room of our house. I was a little tacker, just turned three years of age, but I remember standing on Nan's chair in the lounge room watching the water lap over the carpet and up the walls and couch. As the waters rose, I climbed higher onto the arm of the chair and was standing there when Dad came and scooped me up onto his shoulders and outside into the rain.

A fast-flowing river replaced the concrete and bitumen out in the street, where there were houses on either side. Dad had me on his shoulders as he picked his way along, battling to keep his footing through the torrent as he headed for Aunty Vennie's – our neighbour opposite – on higher ground.

I stayed in Aunty Vennie's kitchen. She was not my blood relative, just a close friend of Mum's. In the 1950s children were encouraged to call adults either by a title – Mr, Mrs or Miss – or make them honorary aunts or uncles.

Aunty Vennie was a very kind and rather glamorous woman in her early 50s. She always wore her blonde hair in a French bun and had the most stylish clothes of anyone in the street. Vennie and her husband, Mark, had no children of their own but welcomed the neighbourhood kids into their house. Mum said that Mark didn't want Vennie to have a child because it would ruin her figure. Mum didn't have much time for Mark. She said he was the kind of neighbour who would borrow but never lend.

Mum stood at our front door with a broom, making frantic, futile attempts to push back the floodwater. Barbara was at the back door with a broom, battling the rising tide.

Dad and Gerald quickly dug a trench to redirect the water running straight from the park, flooding our backyard and flowing into our house. They waded through the rising water and dug in the mud, working as fast as they could. It was an almost hopeless task for one man and a 12-year-old boy. They were desperate for someone to help them but, when they looked up from their daunting task, they could see neighbour Mark, cigarette and beer in hand, observing from the comfort of his verandah.

"Look at him with his chest puffed out like a bloody seagull," said Mum. She had no time for Mark after that.

The event in Gerald's words:
"Dad and I were digging trenches, trying to drain water away from the house. It flooded throughout the house about a foot deep. We stacked things on our beds to keep them dry. Our neighbour Mark Harding over the road was not flooded. He stood watching Dad and I digging for hours and did

nothing. A Salvation Army guy walking through the park saw us digging. He took off his shoes, rolled up his pants and helped, but still, Mark did nothing.

When the swimming rats and flood water finally subsided, there was a huge sinkhole in the middle of the road opposite our house. ... Barbara had waded through that spot earlier that day to cross the road. Dad had carried Maureen over to Vennie's place. How lucky were they? They could have been washed away in the flood.

I remember pulling up the wall-to-wall carpet. Mum got it dry-cleaned. When we put it back it was much smaller. More of a mat than wall-to-wall.

Whenever I think of that day, I don't think of the dramatic circumstances. I think of that sole spectator, Mark Harding. I never liked him after that.

It's times like that you know who your friends are. People with heart – like the Salvos."

When I think back on that time, I can remember Dad's strong arms around me. I remember the panic. I remember the group effort to save the house and as many of our meagre possessions as possible. I remember Aunty Vennie keeping me out of harm's way by baking biscuits with me. I remember our drowned, dead chooks floating in the backyard. Most of all, I remember the devastation on Mum's face – covered in her hands – as Dad put his arms around her.

MAROONED
The Herald Newspaper
December 3, 1954

(In) Fehon Street, fair-haired 10-year-old Barbara Lane waded 300 yards through knee-high flood waters to bring help to her mother and three-year-old sister marooned in their house.

Barbara had just come home from school for lunch when the water began to pour into Fehon Street from the Powell Street reserve drains.

Her mother, Mrs Linda Lane, told her to go to relatives for help.

Bare-footed and without a hat or coat, Barbara waded to her aunt's home in Kingston Street. "I still don't know how Barbara didn't fall into a five-foot-deep hole gouged in the road by floodwaters on her way to my house," the girl's aunt, Mrs D. Heffernan said.

But Barbara wasn't worried this afternoon. Her only concern was that she won't be going to school today. "Mum says there's too much work to do at home here," she said.

CHAPTER 4
Yarraville in the 1950s and '60s

"Make yourself useful. Take this paper bag and a knife and go and find some mushrooms in the park," Mum would say when she was sick of my incessant questions and chatter.

She was often desperate to listen to the fourth race at Flemington on the radio. Her only bit of luxury was a punt on the races on the weekend. She and Dad were small-time punters who liked to take "an interest in the gee-gees," as they called it. Any success they had went to buying us luxuries or would be reinvested at the TAB (Totalisator Agency Board) at the next race meeting.

Mum often got rid of me in imaginative ways when I was being a pest. Sometimes, she would tell me to pick up the acorns from the nature strip outside our house and fill my doll's pram with them. I never thought to ask her why she wanted them. I suspect she waited until my back was turned to tip them out again so I would have more busy work another day when she wanted some peace.

Me ready for church in my fuzzy wuzzy cardigan and my favourite sandals.

Nan would sit on the front verandah keeping one eye on me as she read the morning paper – mostly the obituaries to "see who died." Dad joked that she was checking to see if she was listed.

Mum worked hard to keep us all safe, warm, washed and fed. Each winter's morning, she would put the kindling into the wood oven to start the fire first thing, before she did anything else.

"Wake up sleepyheads," she would say, and I would wipe the sleep from my eyes and crawl over Barbara to get out of bed. If Barbara had been out late the night before and wanted a sleep-in, Mum would get a glass of water and sprinkle a few drops on her face. That always got her up in a hurry. The threat of having the whole glass tipped over any one of us made sure we got up. We didn't believe she would do it, but we weren't really sure. Nobody was ever game to test the theory, though.

Mum was always up early to get Dad his breakfast and start her day. In winter, it was toast and a big, steaming bowl of porridge, sprinkled with sugar and doused in milk for Dad and a smaller serve for each of us. We all wanted the cream off the top of the milk bottle, but Mum sorted the argument by shaking it and mixing the cream through the milk.

The glorious aroma of bacon and eggs often wafted through the window from the Barretts' house next door and into ours. There would be no such luxuries for us. Still, porridge and toast with jam or honey hit the spot. In summer, the porridge was replaced by Cornflakes or Weetbix.

Mum used a poker to stoke the kindling and placed scrunched-up newspaper in the old wood stove. Once the fire caught hold, the kitchen would heat up in time for me to be dressed in front of the glowing embers, which Mum called "fairies" as they sparked and flew up the chimney. A black heavy kettle stayed on top of the stove. It served as water for hot tea and to wash our hands and faces. Our shilling-in-the-meter gas service under our sink was saved for our evening bath. Eventually, we got a new gas stove, but it was never as warm as the old wood stove in the kitchen.

Mum and I enjoyed listening to a serial on the radio in the morning. It was warm in the kitchen after the others had gone to work or school and there was only Mum, Nan and me left. Nan would be hurriedly cleaning up and doing the dishes.

"I like to make myself useful," she would say.

Mum would lift me, aged five, up to stand on the wooden tabletop while she dressed me. The kitchen was cosy, but the rest of the house was icy. Late in the afternoon, the lounge room fire would be lit, ready for Gerald and Barbara to come home from school. Every payday, Dad would bypass the fire and head straight to his bedroom drawer to hide the Darrell Lee chocolates and liquorice he had secreted on his person. They would only be produced after we had eaten our dinner.

Our house was flanked on one side by a park that wound its way around the back of our house. My friend and neighbour Margaret and I spent a lot of time in that park looking for the elusive mushrooms. Of course, Mum didn't care if we found mushrooms or not. It was inevitable that we would get distracted by the playground with its metal slide that sizzled in the sun and burnt our legs as we slid down. Then we would climb the steps again – over and over until our legs were red raw. The see-saw was a big drawcard, too. We sat on each end and went up and down until we felt sick ... always fun. Sometimes we walked along the see-saw or stood in the middle to make the plank go up and down as we shifted our weight from foot to foot. We found fun in the simplest of things.

When Dad wasn't working he was fun. I spent many hours in the garage "helping" him invent or fix things. He was a brilliant inventor and made me a dancing doll to play with, amongst other things.

Dad had a cheeky side and had always been a bit of a daredevil. Fire Cracker

Night, also known as Guy Fawkes Night, brought out the naughty boy in him. This particular time Dad and I were in the backyard. Mum cast an eye over proceedings and disappeared into the kitchen to tackle the dirty dishes in the sink.

"Gerry," she tossed Dad a warning over her shoulder. "Be careful."

Dad and I were in the yard. Dad had a penny bunger in his hand. The fuse sizzled as he clasped the cracker between his thumb and forefinger, held his arm at full stretch to the side and turned his head in the opposite direction.

"BANG!"

The penny bunger exploded into a million red pieces that landed on the ground. Dad was grinning defiantly with the largest remains from the dead fireworks still clutched between his fingers.

Wiping the grin from his face, he feigned a stern look.

"Never do this," Dad said, and he lit the fuse on another cracker, again holding it at arms-length.

"BANG!" His face broke into a big smile.

"Gerry! Don't be so bloody stupid," Mum was on the veranda, and she was cross.

"I had a mate that did that too close and got blinded," Dad said. "I want the kids to know not to do it."

That was the end of the demonstration. Mum marched me back to the safety of the veranda to watch as Dad set rockets whizzing from a Loys' lemonade bottle. They exploded into a kaleidoscope of colour in the sky.

The smell of the gunpowder hung heavy in the air. With the fireworks supply depleted, Dad was left to clean up the mess in the backyard and to try to coax the family dog out from under my bed.

Dad would use the skills of his youth to his advantage when the opportunity arose.

Once a year a travelling carnival set up in the park and caused a great deal of excitement for everyone. It was a major event in Yarraville. It had bright lights, tinny music, the merry-go-round, the shooting gallery and flying horses that swung out on metal rods while kids hung on for dear life trying not to fall off. No seatbelts back then. Just a strong grip on the rods and a prayer.

Dad was a good marksman and won a prize at every shooting gallery at every carnival, circus or show we ever attended. One year, at the carnival in the park, Dad kept buying tickets and winning prizes until the man told him to "Put your money in your pocket and piss off!" All those years in Crowlands shooting rabbits for dinner had paid off.

Yarraville has always had a strong village atmosphere, created in part by the single main street shopping area. The residential, narrow side streets reek of history and the houses are close together, making a small-town feeling, even if the area is quite large and only about 10km from Melbourne's bustling city centre.

The sense of community has not changed much since the 1950s when I was growing up in our modest double-fronted weatherboard. Ours was like the ones built for returning servicemen after World War II, although Dad was prevented from serving because of a severe lung condition he suffered as a child. Yarraville's community spirit may not have changed, but the blue-collar, working-class residents have largely given way to a white-collar, more affluent variety.

As a little tacker, in my pre-school days, I went with Mum to the shops every day to get something to cook for dinner. She knew everyone and we stopped to chat at every opportunity. Mum's favourite shopkeeper was Mary, the Italian lass whose family owned the fruit and vegetable store on Anderson Street, next to the railway lines. Mary had a lovely smile and a warm glow and the two women always chatted and seemed genuinely interested in each other's lives. I think Mary was Mum's only "new Australian" friend, as they were called back then.

Plarre's cake shop was always exciting. Mum bought pound cake when we were expecting a visit from relatives or as a family treat. Pound cake was usually plain cake, orange cake, chocolate cake or marble cake (marbled with food colouring that created patterns in the sponge) and was baked in a long tin, then cut to the size required by the customer. It was weighed and sold by the pound – and ounce.

Sometimes Mum would call me into the lounge room before we went shopping and I would find her kneeling on spread-out newspapers.

"Come and hold these papers. I don't want them to move," she would say. I would hold the corners of our old newspapers that she had saved. Mum had already opened them and smoothed them with her hands before rolling them into cylinder shapes and tying a string around their middle.

"Put your finger on the string, Maureen," Mum would say, and I would feel happy to be able to help while she tied a knot. She placed the cylinders into her shopping jeep, and we would take them to the fish and chip shop where Mum would get some cash for them. I think it was her only spending money. The proprietor would toss his hot fish, chips, potato cakes, dim sims and Chiko Rolls out of the wire cooking basket onto some greaseproof paper atop the newspaper. Then, he would wrap it up like a present.

On one occasion, I remember Mum sitting me on the countertop so I could watch the chips sizzling in the fryer. He was part of a big Greek population that made their homes in Yarraville. The man spoke kindly to me in broken English:

"You good girl to help mummy." I smiled. Then, behind the counter, he wrapped a few chips in a small parcel just for me. I was thrilled. It was the only time I got a packet of chips of my very own.

Fish and chips were mandatory for us Catholics on Friday. It was supposed to be a day of fasting and abstinence – abstaining from meat was supposed to be character-building to practise self-denial, but we did it terribly wrong. It was no hardship to have fish and chips and cake. It was more of a feast day for us than a day of penance.

My Friday visit with Mum to Plarres was thrilling, as that was the night that we had cream cakes for dessert, after our traditional fish and chip dinner. I salivated, with my nose pressed against the glass that showcased delicious treats – cupcakes shaped like green tree frogs, creamy vanilla slices, cream puffs and, my favourite, whipped cream between two dollops of meringue. Dad and I both liked that one best. Mum had to get two of those in her order of "half a dozen assorted cream cakes please," to keep us both happy.

Mum loved Fridays because she didn't have to cook. She enjoyed a day away from the stove. Occasionally on a Saturday night, we got a Chinese meal from Poon's Chinese Restaurant in Footscray.

"Gerry, take the good pots with the tight-fitting lids," she would say, giving Dad a big smile. Dad would take them to Poon's to have them filled with chow mein and fried rice. That was how we had take-away food in the '50s and '60s. BYO saucepans. Nothing to recycle then.

Mum seemed always to be working. Food preparation took up much of the day, even with Nan's help and my well-intentioned hindrance.

She kept the house spotless without being too pedantic. I was allowed to make a mess, so long as I cleaned it up – and make a mess I did. I made mud pies, using Mum's old pans, and tried to get my neighbour Margaret to eat them. She declined. I did experiments with anything I could find in the laundry. With the assistance and at the insistence of my cousin, John Mullins, I made an "ant killer," which never actually killed an ant, but certainly ensured they were spotlessly clean.

All my toys were hand-me-downs from my brother and sister and were piled behind the lounge room door in a doll's pram. I would tip them out on the floor to play with them.

Gerald's contributions to my toy corner were some toy soldiers, a Batmobile and some plastic "cowboys and Indians." These got an especially good workout when cousin John came to visit. Years later, it would be one of the highlights of my travelling life to visit the Navajo in Monument Valley and learn, as an adult, about their culture and customs.

My strongest memory of 50 Fehon Street is that it was full of love. I'm not saying I didn't get into trouble at times for being a bit of a brat, but a smack on the hand and a few minutes in the bathroom –where I sobbed on the edge of the bath reflecting on my bad behaviour – was punishment enough. It was never a hard smack. It was my pride that was hurt more than anything. The door was never locked – it remained half open. Time out was the norm in our house before anyone had ever heard that terminology. After a few minutes and enough tears of repentance, Mum would push the door open. I would get a hug as she accepted my apology and an assurance that "It would never happen again", until the next time. I was always ashamed when I upset my parents. I don't think I ever did anything wrong on purpose.

Mum was the one who dealt out punishment, not Dad. He never smacked me. He was my playmate when I was little. I spent hours sitting next to our old Vanguard car with Dad's legs protruding from under the chassis.

"Hand me the spanner/screwdriver/wrench," he would say, and then he would explain what it looked like. I dutifully passed him the tools and he would work his magic to get the old car back on the road in good running order. Dad gave me a sense of accomplishment by including me.

"She's Daddy's little girl," Mum would say. She was right.

Daddy's little girl.

CHAPTER 5
Family Fun

Dad was always whistling a tune, singing songs, reciting poetry or telling a story. He also played old records like *The Happy Prince*, a story by Oscar Wilde, narrated by Bing Crosby and Orson Welles that was released in 1944 – long before my time. Dad loved that story and, as soon as I heard it begin, I was straight into the lounge room to watch the black disc go around on the record player and to savour those velvety voices as they told the compelling story of *The Happy Prince*. Spoiler alert: It has a sad, but beautiful ending. I would be sobbing, inconsolably, as the music at the end rose and my demeanour plummeted.

"Gerry! Put that bloody thing off! You know it makes her cry!" Mum was not pleased. But, of course, I would beg to hear it again – promising faithfully that I would not cry this time – only to dissolve into a puddle of tears as the words were spoken … *"'Bring me the two most precious things in the city,' said God to one of His angels; and the angel brought Him the leaden heart and the dead bird."*
I still can't get to the end without a lump in my throat and a tear in my eye.

Dad's recitation of *The Wreck of the Hesperus* was also a tearjerker, inciting Mum's wrath from as far away as the kitchen – she really did have good hearing. In that poem, a little girl dies in a shipwreck, lashed to the ship by her father in a futile attempt to keep her safe during a storm at sea. Not a jolly story. Mum didn't like me listening to that, but nobody objected when Dad recited his favourite poem:

The Puppy Dogs' Party

Once the puppy dogs had a party,

They came from near and far.

Some came by motorbike and others came by car.

Before into the ballroom they were allowed to look,

Each dog had to take its backside off and hang it on a hook.

Then when they were seated, every mother, son and sire.

A dirty little poodle dog jumped up and shouted FIRE!

Then all in a scramble, not caring where to look,

Each dog grabbed a backside off any bloomin' hook.

That's why today a dog will leave a nice juicy bone,

To go and sniff a backside that might have been his own.

That was always a hit at any party or gathering, and I have carried on the tradition of reciting *The Puppy Dogs' Party* at every opportunity.

Sunday was the day we would all go out for a drive in the car and Dad would have a captive audience for his comical songs about Aladdin loving a princess or *Old Man Blue Beard*. I wish I could remember them all, but the mists of time have whisked those songs away.

The planets had to align before we could go anywhere in the old car. All these things had to happen without incident:

1. We had to dress in our finest, with hats and gloves, to attend Sunday Mass.
2. Mum would cook a roast lunch – usually lamb with roasted potatoes, roasted pumpkin, peas and gravy.
3. While Mum and Nan prepared the feast, Dad often took me to Williamstown where we fed stale bread to the swans on The Strand or played hide and seek in the old wheat stores near the Time Ball Tower. We could also watch the big ships coming into Port Melbourne across the bay.
4. When our lunch plates were clean, and every morsel of gravy mopped up with some bread and butter, the dishes had to be done. It was my job to dry the forks and spoons and put them away. Not the knives – I couldn't be trusted to do that safely.

Mum and Nan would bustle out of their aprons and into the car and off we would go on an adventure. On more than one occasion, we would rush outside to see Dad with his head under the bonnet and our hearts would sink.

"What's wrong, Ged?" – that was her nickname for Dad.

"Nothing, Lin. Just checking the oil and water," and we would all heave a collective sigh of relief.

Sunday afternoon drives often included foraging for food that supplemented our diets. Blackberry season was a particular favourite of mine. We would drive into the countryside with buckets and bowls in the boot of the car. Someone would spot some wild blackberry bushes on the side of the road and Dad would stop the car. We would pick the juicy blackberries and carefully place them into the bucket or bowl so they wouldn't get squashed. I had my own way of picking blackberries. One in the bucket and one in my mouth – one in the bucket and two in my mouth and repeat until the bush was bare of ripe berries. Of course, my greed resulted in disaster on the way home as the car wended its way through the countryside, over bumps and bridges, and there was the inevitable:

"Mum. I feel sick."

Mum was oblivious to my usual system of picking blackberries, until one day when I had doubled down on my blackberries, which led to me doubling over on the side of the road. Mum held back my long curls and let out a yell.

"Gerry! She's haemorrhaging!" On closer inspection the problem became clear.

As Mum tucked me into bed, she wagged her finger:

"You won't do that again, will you?" There was no chance of that. I had lost my taste for blackberries … until the next time.

Our most memorable attempt at foraging in the countryside involved mushrooms as big as side plates. It was a cold day, but the sun was shining so Mum, Dad, Nan and I bundled into the car and took off towards Bacchus Marsh, west of our home in Yarraville.

Dad drove through the back roads scouring the paddocks for a likely spot to find mushrooms growing wild. He searched for a spot that met all the criteria. First, he looked for winter green grass with longish, dead stalks, which meant a farmer had not recently mowed. He wanted it to be out of view of passing cars and, most importantly, nowhere near a farmer's cottage.

There it was.

Dad pulled the car over to the roadside and got the buckets and knives out of the boot. A barbed-wire fence surrounded a lush, green paddock. A big rock next to one of the poles could act as a stile to make climbing over the wire a bit easier.

"Perfect," Dad said, as he cleared the wire in one jump and bent down to hold the barbs apart so Mum could step through. Next, I got through the gap and Dad let the two strands of wire spring back into place. Nan sat dozing in the back seat of the car. She never engaged in any foraging. She did, however, prepare the bounty to be eaten when the time came.

Once we were in the paddock, Mum looked warily.

"I don't like the look of those bulls, Gerry."

"Don't worry," Dad replied. "See the fence that separates this paddock from theirs?" Mum nodded and we spread out to search for mushrooms. It wasn't long before the call of "Got some!" rang out.

The bulls in the next paddock began to take notice of us and became restless, but we continued running from mushroom to mushroom.

"I've never seen such big mushies. They are big as bread-and-butter plates." Mum was excited and mentally preparing them for cooking – on toast, in stews, as sauce.

"Oh shit!" Dad's voice had a sense of urgency. "Don't run. Just start walking back to the fence."

"What's wrong, Ged?" Mum asked.

"That fence between the two paddocks ends halfway," Dad answered, trying to keep his voice calm.

"Just don't run and we'll be all right. Walk. We don't want them chasing us."

Mum looked at the bulls just a short distance from her and she took off as fast as she could. The bulls quickened their pace. I saw her run and my little legs carried me as fast as they would go. Dad knew there was nothing to do but run now, so he sprinted towards the fence, overtook us both and got there first. He nimbly jumped over and started to help Mum get through the wire, but her dress became tangled on the barbs. She was stuck and I was still on the same side of the fence as the bulls. I tried to help by planting my two hands on her bottom and pushing her.

"Ow. Don't help." Mum's voice was panicked but not as much as mine.

"They're coming and I can't get my foot on the rock until you move," I said as I kept shoving her bottom as hard as I could. This was self-preservation.

We must have looked a comical sight: Dad with one foot on the barbs and a hand holding up another piece of wire; Mum bent over with one leg through the fence and her other foot on the rock that acted as a stile; and little me, with both hands planted firmly on her rear end pushing with all my weight.

Somehow Mum made it through, and Dad's hand reached over the fence and grabbed me by the coat, lifting me to safety in the nick of time.

The bulls lost interest immediately and went about their business. We recovered in the car, laughing nervously at our adventure. We would retell the tale of "The Running of the Bulls" for many years to come.

Home Is Where the Heart Is

Our house was pretty crowded in the early 1960s. Mum and Dad had the main bedroom at the front of the house; Nan, Barbara and I shared the middle bedroom; and Gerald had a narrow room built on the end of the back verandah.

It was pretty squashed in that middle bedroom. Barbara and I shared a double bed while Nan had a single. There was a double wardrobe, an old dressing table and a chest of drawers as well in that room. When Pam, Gerald's girlfriend, stayed overnight, she slept on a mattress on the floor in our room, too. It was quite a crush. The door to our room had dressing gowns hung on hooks on the back. They would have prevented the door from shutting if it wasn't for the dressing table that was already in the way. As I lay in the darkened room at night, I would watch those dressing gowns on the back of the door, just in case they moved. My overactive imagination was probably fuelled by the latest *Alfred Hitchcock Presents* episode on TV. It always scared the pants off me, but I wouldn't let Mum know or she wouldn't let me watch it next week.

The double bed was a constant source of squabbles between Barbara and me. She would roll over and wrap the blankets around herself in the night, leaving me with only a sheet. I complained to Mum that Barb pulled the blankets off me, and Mum settled the matter by buying two huge safety pins (the kind worn in kilts) and pinning the blankets to the mattress. This was a great success until Barb rolled over in the night, taking the blankets and a chunk out of the mattress.

We all got along pretty well, considering we lived in such proximity to each other. I must have annoyed Barbara a bit, though I can't remember what I did. I do remember her light-hearted taunt about my curly hair:

"There was a little girl,
who had a little curl,
right in the middle of her forehead.
When she was good,
she was very, very good,
but when she was bad,
she was horrid."

Nan was everybody's idea of the ideal grandmother. Short, round, cuddly, jolly and kind ... with a secret stash of lollies hidden in her drawer. When Barbara was watching TV, visiting Silhouette Figure Control Studio or out at the movies, all would be quiet in our room. There was darkness, except for the hall light. I was scared of the dark – all those dressing gowns on the door were coming to get me. Nan was in her bed. I was in mine. Then the "rustle, rustle" of paper.

"Nan?" I'd whisper. "Have you got lollies?"

"No," she'd mumble through her teeth (clenched around a Fantale).

"Are you sure?"

"Oh, all right. Here," she'd say, tossing one to me. "Don't tell your mother or you'll get me into all sorts of trouble."

Nan would eat lollies in bed. She had false teeth so brushing was not an issue for her, but her generosity with toffees in bed at night probably accounted for most of my fillings.

Nan at her surprise 80th birthday party.

She was my friend and confidante when I was growing up. She always made me feel like I was helping her as she sat on the front verandah to watch the world go by, shelling the peas or cutting up the beans. She never got angry at my incessant chatter, and she made me feel useful by accepting my help.

Her other jobs around the house included cleaning the fireplace each morning. She would sweep all the embers and soot into a metal bucket and tip it on the garden. One day, Mum bought a new, blue plastic bucket which she proudly showed to us. We were used to the old metal one, and this bright-coloured, sparkling addition to our cupboards seemed very flash indeed. Nan took the bucket to the fireplace, carefully swept up all the grime and tipped the lot into the new bucket. She used her hands to help her get off her knees into an upright position before picking up the embers for garden distribution.

As she took the handle and raised the bucket … CRASH! The entire contents spilled all over the lounge room floor. A dust cloud rose to the ceiling and settled over every piece of furniture. The embers had burnt the base right out of that plastic bucket and there was soot everywhere. Nan was so upset, but Mum and I could see the funny side of it, and we were both able to relate the story many times thereafter, much to Nan's embarrassment. "New-fangled plastic," she said.

The lounge room was my playroom. My place of entertainment. There was a huge old couch, two matching chairs and Nan's lounge chair, which was positioned behind the door. That lounge suite was a toy for me. I used to sit on the arm of the chair and ride my "horse" to Texas, fighting baddies all the way. Alternatively, the broom made a more mobile mount that I galloped outside and into the backyard. The cushions made a tipi, a train or a wagon, and, when all else failed, there was my toy stash hidden behind Nan's chair. In it, there was an array of characters that I would become by simply holding them in my hand.

As I held a toy, I *became* Batman in his Batmobile, a soldier fighting the baddies, the cavalry, an "Indian," a gangster in an old car and, of course, Barbie and my assortment of homemade outfits for her. There were never any store-bought dresses for my Barbie, other than the one she came in. I made her clothes from Dad's old hankies, scraps of lace torn from Mum's old petticoat or a piece of discarded ribbon from one of Barbara's headbands.

There was also a pianola to be played in the early days. Everyone in the family and visitors alike had a go at pumping the pedals to make music, but my legs weren't long enough to reach. The pianola really belonged to Dad. He had the strongest legs and the strongest will to play. Dad loved music and taught himself to play by ear. He only had to hear a tune and he could play it on the piano.

There always seemed to be plenty to do in the lounge room, but in the corner was my favourite thing, the television.

I am a child of the TV era. I remember when we first got our television set. The neighbours came in to watch our little black-and-white box in the corner. Margaret, from two doors up the road, would arrive every night after she had her dinner and announce:

"I can stay 'til half pasty eight." Mum always stifled a laugh at her pronunciation. Margaret's parents were quite rich by our standards, as she was an only child and both her parents worked, but still, they had no TV and sent Margaret to our place every night. Mum got a bit sick of it.

"If they want a babysitter, why don't they just say so? Every night is a bit much."

Mum still made her supper and a cup of tea before she went home at half past eight, though. Every single night. Mum was kind-hearted and didn't refuse anyone her hospitality, even when she felt used.

My favourite TV programs were heavily influenced by Mum. She loved old movies and British comedies, including the *Carry On* movies, and we watched those together. Mum had her favourite TV shows, but her particular favourite genre of TV and movies was the "cowboy." Our favourites were *Sugarfoot, Bronco Lane, Cheyenne, Bonanza, Paladin, Rin Tin Tin, Fury, The Rifleman* and *Circus Boy*. Was it any wonder that my dramatic play mostly centred around cowboys?

Mum's absolute favourite crush was Clint Walker, the star of *Cheyenne*.

"Oh, he's lovely," she would say. Then we would all tease Mum and have the discussion.

"Will he take his shirt off this week?" The muscle-bound star took his shirt off so often that the question became not will he appear bare-chested but how long into the episode would we have to wait before he took his shirt off. When the inevitable happened, Mum would pretend to fan her face with a handkerchief and feel faint at the sight of his rippling muscles. It became quite a joke in the Lane household.

A visit to the movies continued to be a special part of my childhood and became more of a treat. Every school holiday period brought a big day out with Mum in the city to have lunch at Coles' cafeteria and see a movie in town. I remember holding her hand tightly as we crossed at the traffic lights with people streaming towards me. I was invisible to the onslaught of pedestrians, intent on their destination, with never a downward glance to see a terrified child grasping her mother's hand. The crossing became quite an obstacle course as I tried to avoid being stepped on or knocked to the ground.

CHAPTER 6
Saturday Night at the Movies

Yarraville of the 2020s is home to television and movie celebrities and has the art deco Sun Theatre as its jewel in the crown. It originally opened in 1938 and was a single-screen 1050-seat cinema – the most luxurious in the area. Today's Sun Bookshop was the original lolly shop. Inside the lobby, one wall is adorned with telegrams from famous Hollywood actors received when it first opened its doors. The Sun was a huge part of my childhood and is a place I still visit regularly.

The films they showed were mostly family films – family comedies, westerns and thrillers. There were fewer genres to choose from back then. This was because the movie houses of old all had a single screen, so they showed movies with the most appeal to a wide variety of age groups. Now, The Sun and most cinemas have multiple screens in different rooms, so they can have more specialised genres and cater to a variety of audiences.

From the time before I was born, Mum and Dad had permanent seat bookings for every Friday and Saturday night at The Sun or in Footscray at The Grand or The George. I remember promising faithfully one winter's night that I would not cry if Mum and Dad took me to see *Old Yeller*. Spoiler alert: It was a tear-jerker film about a pet dog that had to be shot at the end of the movie. I kept my promise at The Sun that night by biting my lip through the movie and all the way home. As soon as I got through the front door, I flung myself onto my bed and sobbed uncontrollably for hours. Mum was angry and said she would never take me to the movies again, but she did. We went to see *How the West Was Won*. It was a blockbuster that packed the theatre and we had to sit in the front row. Now that film was in CinemaScope, and we were so close I felt as if I was right in the action. When the scene came where the characters were washed down the rapids on a raft, I felt seasick. The rapids scene seemed to go on forever with the hapless characters buffeted by the raging river. I could take it no longer. I threw up all over the floor.

Our frequent trips to the movies ended when we got a TV. I suspect that my performance at *How the West Was Won* might have contributed to the decision.

Saturday night at the movies continued to be a national pastime in the 1950s and '60s for courting couples who snuggled and groped in the darkened theatre. It was often the only place they could go courting, as most people lived at home with their parents until they married.

I remember Barbara going on a date with one of the neighbourhood boys, John. Mum and Dad knew his family, so she was allowed to go to The Sun to see a film on a Saturday night. John worked at the shoe shop in Anderson Street. He picked her up from home and was subjected to the third degree by Dad.

John was given strict instructions by Dad: "Bring her home straight after the movie, and don't be hanging around the streets."

John glanced up at the rifle hanging over the fireplace and enthusiastically nodded: "Yes, Mr Lane."

In the darkened theatre watching the movie, Barbara was a little nervous as he held her hand and then slipped his arm around her shoulder. He was a bit shorter than her, so it was a bit of a reach, she said later.

Courting couples were kissing and snuggling together in the seats around them, but John had taken Dad's words to heart and kept his lips at a distance. That rifle, although it was only for providing rabbit dinners, had the desired effect.

At the end of every movie, the national anthem was played and everyone was supposed to stand up until God had saved the Queen.

That was the theory anyway. In practice, when the music began, there would be a stampede for the door and only staunch royalists and conservatives were left standing – some with hands on their hearts. At the end of the movie, John took off straight out the door, leaving Barb standing until the end of the anthem. She couldn't see him in the crowd outside. John had disappeared. Barbara made her way home on her own.

Barbara was to go on a couple of dates with other boys, but when Gordon Cameron came to pick her up for a night at the drive-in, I knew it was serious.

I don't know how it happened or why, but I got to go with them to the drive-in to watch a movie called *Love is a Ball*, which starred Barbara's heartthrob, Glenn Ford. I suspect it was Mum and Dad's idea to send me as a chaperone. I doubt the courting couple wanted a kid along for the ride.

I sat in the back seat with a blanket over me. I think I was supposed to go to sleep. I was bored enough, that's for sure. The movie was way above my level of understanding, so I concentrated on watching the couple in the front seat. When they shot a glance my way, I closed my eyes. When they turned to the screen, I was wide-eyed, although I couldn't see much. Just an arm slipped around a shoulder and a snuggle or two. Then a noise like a dying bull filled the car.

"Your eyes are the eyes of a woman in love ..." My brother-in-law-to-be was singing a love song. He was smitten, and his advances were welcomed.

I'm not quite sure what happened next. I might have laughed out loud. I know I wasn't allowed to move for the rest of the movie. I lay under a blanket plotting what I would report to Mum when I got home.

I was allowed to go to the "flicks" on Saturday afternoon with our neighbour, Margaret. She was a year older, and I was placed in her care for an afternoon of Sun Theatre movie adventure. No cuddlers and gropers at the Saturday afternoon sessions – just lots of kids laughing and squealing their way through comedies, musicals or cowboy flicks.

We called the movies the flicks because of the reel-to-reel film that sometimes slowed, making a flickering image on the screen. Sometimes, the film would get stuck in the projector and we all watched a frame burn from the middle of the screen outwards and disappear, leaving a blank screen. All the kids would "boo" and stamp their feet on the bare floorboards until the harassed projectionist got the film up and running again.

Every Saturday afternoon, we would settle into the hard, brown leather seats to watch a cartoon, followed by a short – usually a 10-minute comedy that began with "Here's Joe ..." Poor Joe was always trying to fix things and getting into a hopeless mess. He was the worst handyman ever, and we laughed raucously at his antics.

Then would come the serial, which was usually a cowboy with a story that would continue the next week. It always finished with an imminent disaster – the stagecoach carrying the hero or heroine would plummet over the cliff and smash to smithereens. The audience would let out an audible gasp or scream followed by a collective "Boo." The next week, it would be revealed that the hero or heroine had jumped from the stagecoach just before it went over the cliff – always just in the nick of time. The audience would either breathe a sigh of relief or give an audible groan at being tricked ... again.

An "intermission" sign would flash onto the screen and there would be a scramble to get to the lolly counter.

I was allowed 2/6 to go to the Saturday matinee at The Sun each week. I'd buy lollies with the change: a toffee for tuppence, a penny each for a musk stick and a Sherbet Bomb, sixpence for a White Knight or Choo Choo Bar. One penny also bought either six blocks or a strap of liquorice.

It was a big decision. This was my only spending money. The way I would spend it was considered long and hard. The longevity of a lolly was usually the deciding factor. A musk stick I could make last the entire main feature as I twisted the end around and around in my pursed lips, making a point. A liquorice strap could be stripped into fine lengths, lasting a long time. Toffees with coconut on top not only lasted the distance but there was a chance of a lucky threepence hidden in the base. I got a lucky one once and ran straight to the lolly counter for a feast, which I shared with Margaret.

I have always loved the movies. The excitement of going to escape into another world has fascinated me. Sitting in the darkness of the theatre, I lived the roles on the screen. Musicals such as *Seven Brides for Seven Brothers*, *Tom Thumb*, *Singin' in the Rain*, *Brigadoon* and *Li'l Abner* had me singing and dancing all the way home.

As soon as I walked through our door, I would race into the laundry and raid my dress-up box, get into my mum's abandoned blue lace petticoat and out into the backyard where I re-enacted each movie, scene by scene. The clothesline was my leading man, and I would dance around with my co-star "Singin' in the Rain" or snuggle up to plant a big kiss on the silver metal. "Oh, Rhett. Where will I go and what shall I do?" In my version of *Gone with the Wind*, Rhett didn't resist Scarlett's charms and they lived happily ever after, skipping off into the sunset ... behind the chook shed.

Woah there, partner: Me in the backyard at Fehon Street, Yarraville where I acted out every film from beginning to end, using all the dress ups I could find. Minor roles were played by our dog, Darkie and the clothesline.

Wanna Bet?

Saturday afternoon movies also provided an escape from the constant drone of the horse races being called over our radio every Saturday afternoon. Mum and Dad both continued to like a bet on the horses, and I think they were glad to get rid of me for a while.

One of my earliest memories is of the "woodie" tossing logs of wood over the fence from the back of his truck as it idled in the park. Mum would go and talk to him at the fence and he would flirt with her.

"Looking lovely as ever, Linda."

Mum would laugh and reach into her apron pocket to retrieve a 10-shilling note and pass it to him in exchange for a piece of paper. I always thought Mum was paying for the wood until much later when I discovered that the woodie was an SP bookie and Mum was placing bets for herself and Dad.

As I got a bit older, Mum would send me up the street to the dry-cleaning shop on Anderson Street. I did think it was odd that I never picked up any dry-cleaning. The proprietor of the drycleaners was running a "book" on the side as an SP bookie.

Very occasionally, we would go to the trotting races at night. The lights made the sandy track glisten and the air was always full of excited expectation. Punters studying the form guide from the *Sporting Globe* or *The Sun News-Pictorial* newspapers would be trying to pick a winner from the list of horses trotting along pulling lightweight carriages with lightweight jockeys behind them. The bookies, with their big shoulder bags full of money, waving tickets in the air, fascinated me. "Five bob on number two in the fourth," someone would shout, waving his cash up high. That was snatched, checked and a ticket issued with a black scribble on it.

The lights and the excitement made it a fun night out for me. I also liked collecting the discarded tickets from the ground and playing with them. Dad used to check them, making sure a winner had not been thrown away in error. There never was.

Both Mum and Dad were "50 cents each-way" punters – if the horse won or came second or third, they collected some money. It was really their only vice. Except for the occasional shandy when we had guests.

Dad loved the horses. From the old nags on the farm at Crowlands to the sleek racehorses and trotters at the track. They were beautiful creatures. His father had lived near North Melbourne stables when he was a kid, watching the racehorses come and go. Dad's love of horses was probably inherited from him.

One night, when we were at the trots, Mum prodded me, "Look over there. It's King Corky from *The Tarax Show*." I watched that show every afternoon. I loved Happy Hammond and Princess Panda, and Geoff "King" Cork was a frequent participant in what was a daily kids' cartoon show. I was excited to see him in the flesh even though he wasn't wearing his crown. Mum and Dad pushed me forward with a piece of paper and pen to ask "the king" for his autograph. I was overawed but managed to ask politely, remembering my manners. King Corky obliged with a smile but without conversation.

As we walked away, with me clutching the prized autograph, we heard his wife say disdainfully, "How disgusting. Fancy bringing a child to the trots."

Mum was very upset: "I'll bet she left her kids home with other people to look after them. Not everyone has servants."

Mum remained quite angry and upset all evening and into the next week. It was very seldom that Mum and Dad got to go anywhere, and they never left their children at home. On this rare occasion, they had a family night out and she felt chastised for it.

The Tarax Show ran from 1957 to 1970. It was a mixture of comedy sketches and cartoons hosted by Happy Hammond, who wore a distinctive tartan coat and hat and a small Errol Flynn-style moustache. 'Happy' ran a segment where he sat in the audience of children and asked them to tell him a joke. On one occasion, the cast and crew were stunned by the joke offered by a small boy.

Child: "Why didn't Popeye's pipe ever go rusty?

Happy: "I don't know; why didn't Popeye's pipe ever go rusty?"

Child: "Because he was always dipping it in Olive Oil."

The screen went to blank and they cut to an ad break.

Jingle Bells

Christmas with the Lanes was a magical time and always involved a trip to the city on a "red rattler" train with Mum, where we had lunch at Myer's cafeteria and visited Santa.
"Hold onto my hand," Mum warned, "You'll fall."
With those words, she successfully instilled in me a lifelong fear of escalators. I clung to her hand as we ascended to the place where the elves had prepared a red and golden throne for Santa to receive his fans. A line of excited children snaked around through the toy aisles, up to the foot of the platform that held Santa's chair, where the man himself perched regally, welcoming each child with open arms, a big smile and a huge "Ho, ho, ho." When it was my turn, Mum let go of my hand and gave me a little push forward indicating, "Off you go, sit on his knee," and I obliged. I was always very shy. I managed to smile at the camera and whispered into Santa's ear that I had indeed been a good little girl and deserved a gift on Christmas morning.
On one such visit to see the jolly gentleman in red, I whispered that I wanted a bride doll. Santa shot a glance at Mum.
"Are you sure you want a bride doll?" he asked, questioningly.
Mum slightly nodded her head.
"I will do my very best to get a bride doll to you on Christmas morning. Don't forget to be kind to your family and be a good girl," he responded.
Off I skipped, hand in hand with Mum, through the crowded stores and home on the train. We would return the next night with Dad, Nan, Barbara and Gerald to view the Christmas dioramas that graced the Myer windows. The Bourke Street windows each depicted a page from a book, ballet or fairy tale, with moving parts that brought them to life.
The Myer Christmas windows hold a special place in the heart of most Melburnians. I recall with fond nostalgia gazing through the glass at each window, jostling to the front of the crowd so I could see past the adults who enjoyed this magical display as much as the kids. If the crowd was too enthusiastic to let in a little kid, though, Dad put me on his shoulders so I could see.
One smaller window was always reserved for a nativity scene: Mary and Joseph with baby Jesus in the manger. That was the most magical of all. The figures were grand and sparkling, not at all like the simple nativity under our Christmas tree. Mum would take my hand in hers gently and say, "Don't forget the real meaning. It's baby Jesus' birthday and we have to be kind to everyone. That's the gift we can give Him."
Christmas Eve meant midnight Mass. The carols filled a darkened St Augustine's Church, and there was a warm inner glow mixed with a buzz of anticipation.

Sometimes the priest managed to dispel all the goodwill with a sermon admonishing those who only made it to Mass at Christmas and Easter. That has always made the hairs on my arms stand up. I believed then, as I do now, that everyone is welcome in a church.

Now there is a new breed of priests who welcome everyone to the manger – from the shepherds (ruffians and the poor) to the wise men (intellectuals and the rich). Everyone should share in the peace and joy of Christmas. It's the gathering that makes the whole Christmas experience a spiritual one, not commercialism.

After midnight Mass, the crowd spilled onto the street to wish strangers goodwill with a wave or a handshake or a hearty "Merry Christmas." The air was filled with something undefinable, but I will do my best to explain how midnight Mass makes me feel. It is a kind of belonging to a collective of peace and gratitude, mixed with quiet anticipation. It's about being connected to love through a story of acceptance.

As soon as I was home, I was straight into bed.

"Go to sleep quickly so Santa can come," Mum said as she tucked me in.

Nan chimed in, "Good night. Sleep tight. It's a big day tomorrow." I was asleep as soon as my head hit the pillow.

Bride dolls were very expensive and probably quite a bit over our family budget, but Mum was on the lookout for a bargain in the damaged-and-seconds bin of any retail outlet. She was in charge of the finances in our house and could work magic on even the smallest budget.

When I woke on Christmas morning, a beautiful blonde bride doll was sitting on the bed at my feet. I was ecstatic. On closer inspection, I found that my new doll had a big Band-Aid on her shoulder. "Santa dropped her when he was getting down the chimney," Mum explained. The crack in her shoulder mattered not a jot. My new doll was perfect to me.

On another Christmas morning, I awoke to find a doll's pram at the foot of my bed. It was Barbara's hand-me-down pram, as I mentioned before, but Dad had painted it shiny black and adorned it with colourful stickers. I was none the wiser and made good use of my "new" pram by putting our fox terrier, Rusty, into it and parading him around the yard dressed in a baby bonnet with ribbons tied under his chin. The hat did not last even once around the yard before it was dislodged and abandoned somewhere in the geranium bushes. Rusty suffered a good many indignities, but that was one step too far.

Christmas lunch was roast chickens – a rare treat indeed. We only had chickens at Christmas and Easter. They didn't fit the everyday budget, but during the festive season, it made a lunch special. Roast potatoes, peas and beans, carrots, roasted pumpkin and gravy. Followed by plum pudding laced with silver coins to bring us luck. There was ham and salad for dinner and Mum's famous trifle, too. Aunty Pat and Uncle Frank came for dinner and brought us presents and some treats. Glazed fruits were a luxury that I had not sampled until Pat and Frank introduced me to them one Christmas. Then they became a tradition.

Dad always got walnuts at Christmas and cracked them with a nutcracker or hammer. He made his nutcracker, which was shaped like a crocodile and snapped the shells between its jaws. He would spend much of the afternoon cracking the nuts for himself and others. Walnuts, almonds and occasionally hazelnut shells were used as mulch in the garden.

The evening would be spent playing Twister, Ludo or card games before settling in to watch Christmas movies on the TV. *White Christmas* was a favourite of Mum's – she loved Bing Crosby. After such a big day, I was probably a bit cranky, so I was sent to bed early. Nan fell asleep in the chair and the house exuded contentment.

As I got a bit older, our Christmas was moved to a holiday destination – the beach or the bush. The essence of the holy day was much the same but with different scenery and a lot more excitement.

Summer Holidays

"Oh, Gerry. What have you got there?" Mum's voice showed her exasperation.

Dad and Uncle Frank were laughing the laugh of cheeky boys up to mischief as they manoeuvred a newly felled Christmas tree through the narrow lounge room door of our country holiday rental in the hills of Cockatoo, in the Dandenong Ranges.

The Lane family had one holiday each year – compliments of Nan's pension cheque. She lived with us and saved her money to provide us with a yearly treat.

My parents never travelled on an aeroplane to a holiday destination. It was out of the reach of any blue-collar working family, but, through the generosity of my Nan, we drove to a holiday destination at Christmas. She had little money, but what she had she shared with us. One year, our destination would be the countryside or bushland; the next it would be the seaside.

This particular year, it was an old wooden house, surrounded by lush, green forests and the clean, fresh smell of pine trees. It was a far cry from the working-class suburban community of Yarraville in the 1950s and '60s.

Mum, Dad, Nan, Barbara, Gerald and I had squashed into our old Vanguard, and the family dog was plonked on top of us. Luggage was piled atop the roof racks and balanced precariously as Dad manoeuvred around the winding roads without incident. Uncle Frank and Aunty Pat were to arrive later.

Cockatoo was a lovely country town, just 48km south-east of Melbourne. Its leafy green forestation was, and still is, a big attraction for those of us who lived in more commercialised and populated city areas.

For Mum, it was a change of scenery but not much of a holiday. She still did most of the cooking, cleaning and washing.

That first night, after the dishes were done, we settled down in front of the 17-inch black and white TV to watch a Christmas movie together. Instead, though, Dad and Uncle Frank hatched a plan. They disappeared in the car and returned half an hour later.

"Gerry! Oh no! You didn't!" Mum was used to Dad's mischief, but this was just too much. Dad and Uncle Frank were struggling, coaxing and shoving a stolen Christmas tree through the door. Crash! They overbalanced and ended up on their backsides, laughing raucously.

"I can't believe you stole a tree at Christmas. You'll both go to hell," Mum railed. The boys looked sheepishly at each other and stifled a smile.

"It's done now," Mum continued. "Just put it in the corner and come and sit down. *Miracle on 34th Street* is on the television and we are missing it."

They did as they were told and settled down with the family to watch the movie, ignoring the mess of pine needles and wood chips strewn on the carpet.

I was the first to notice it. A slight movement in the dark.

"Mum. That wood chip moved."

"Don't be silly," Mum dismissed me. The movie was still on.

"It moved again," I insisted.

Dad got up and put the light on. There, strewn over the floor, was a colony of tiny lizards frozen by the light – until I let out a squeal.

The lizards took off in every direction. Barbara screamed and tucked her legs up on the seat. Gerald sprang to his feet and chased the lizards, zig-zagging around the floor. Mum yelled at Dad. Aunty Pat cursed Uncle Frank. Mayhem exploded like a Marx Brothers movie as frightened lizards were pursued, quickly taking refuge in every nook and cranny.

From my vantage point, standing on the arm of the lounge chair, it was all very exciting.

As our hearts slowed and order crept back through the house, Mum chastised Dad.

"That's what you get for thieving. You should have had more sense." The two men shot sideways glances at each other and stifled a laugh as they dragged the tree into the backyard.

Our accidental house guests had scattered. The boys sheepishly swept up the pine chips, eyes downcast and heads bowed, but lips were bitten and shoulders shuddering.

Christmas Day came and went. Dad and Uncle Frank's adventure with the stolen tree and its inhabitants had been forgiven, if not forgotten.

We ate too much, drank too much and had a great time. We all squashed into that three-bedroom house and overindulged in the way most of us do during the Christmas season, but, as we all know, what goes in must come out, and the toilet pan filled up.

Now, with the sanitation worker – the pan man – on Christmas holidays, it was up to Dad and Uncle Frank to find a solution to the um ... rising problem. There was only one course of action.

Mum, Barbara, Nan, Gerald, Aunty Pat and I stood way back on the verandah watching. Comically dressed with ladies' scarves around their noses in a futile attempt to block the stench, Dad and Uncle Frank struggled with the full pan that splashed with every step.

They laughed and stumbled as they carried that pan the full width of the backyard before dumping the contents into a hole.

From the safety of the verandah, we all shouted and cheered, doubled up with laughter and tears streaming down our cheeks as they shovelled dirt into the hole, jumping backwards to avoid random splashes.

As the two men sheepishly sauntered towards the garden hose for a thorough dousing, Mum yelled, "Let that be your penance for pinching a tree ... and at Christmas too!"

A Christmas holiday to remember. From left, back row: Uncle Frank, Gerald and his visiting friend Richard. Middle: Barbara, Mum. Front: Me, Nan and Auntie Pat.

The next year, we booked a house in the bayside suburb of Chelsea, which has a straight and uninterrupted stretch of coastline with scenic views towards the Mornington Peninsula. The neighbouring beaches of Edithvale and Bonbeach were as safe for swimming, and many happy hours were spent on our blow-up rubber inner tube car tyres or the polystyrene boogie boards that we surfed on in the waves.

"Have you got everything?" Mum's voice echoed through the empty house as we dragged bags, boxes and linen into the driveway, only to be greeted with the sight of Dad's legs sticking out from under the car. Our hearts sank again. What was wrong with the car this time? We were going to Chelsea beach for a whole week and did not want to miss a minute.

"Just have to check the brake fluid." Dad's words brought a collective sigh of relief. Too many times we had hurriedly gotten ready for a Sunday drive to find out that Dad had the car in pieces in the driveway searching for that elusive "squeak" he'd been listening to all week.

We piled into the old Vanguard – Mum, Dad, Barbara, Nan and me. Gerald, my big brother, would drive down with his friend Richard, Aunty Pat and Uncle Frank.

Nan had been waiting in the car for the past half hour, anxious to be on her way but never saying a word. She was a short, rotund woman with white permed hair, and as I rounded the back of the car, I giggled at how much Nan resembled a French poodle through the back window. I wondered how many excited little kids would be disappointed as they rode past us, realising that the anticipated poodle was only an old lady's frizzy, white hair.

We all tried to make ourselves comfortable for the long drive, but the seat was sizzling hot and we complained and laughed about our bottoms sticking to the seats.

Nan was the only one who didn't complain. Her summer dress was pulled down over her ample, dimpled knees to cover the tops of her stockings that were held in place with knicker elastic loops under those knees. No flesh of hers would sizzle on those seats.

Why does it always seem to take longer to get to your destination than to return home? It seemed to take forever to start our holiday, travelling bumper to bumper down the two-lane roads in the traffic from Yarraville to Chelsea. There was no West Gate Bridge in the 1950s, so we had to go through Melbourne to get to Chelsea. It seemed so much further away then.

The house in Bristol Avenue was a modest weatherboard with an outside toilet and washhouse that doubled as a bathroom. No mod cons here. The big saving grace was its location – just a few houses from the beach.

"What do you want a bathroom for? There's the whole beach out there to swim in." Dad was happy. The rest of the family wasn't so sure. Right away, Dad decided he would swim every day – rain, hail but, hopefully, shine. I promised to go with him.

The Chelsea house had quite a few beds, but the first order of the day was to set up mattresses on the floor. There were so many of us that there were never enough beds in the rental houses that Nan could afford. Rubber mattresses were preferable to blow-up ones because they were cooler and the sheets didn't keep slipping. There was also a baby's cot that we tucked out of the way in a cul-due-sac beside the front door. The door mostly stayed open to catch any passing breath of cool air and the cot was out of sight.

I tagged along with Dad everywhere. He never spoke to me like I was a child or indicated he thought I wouldn't understand. He always treated me as an equal, teaching me things as we walked. With my hand in his, we took the footpath to the milk bar every morning to get the newspaper and milk. We would walk back along the beach. The trip there was sometimes boring for me, as the cars zoomed past, but Dad pointed out items of interest as we went.

Inevitably, I would get distracted or tired and start to drag my feet. It was then that Dad brought out the old army marching chants to pick up my pace:

"I had a good job for 50-bob

"But I hit the manager in the gob and I

"Left-left, left-right-left."

Or the rhyme that was, to my mind, a bit risqué and always made me giggle:

"Ask your mother for sixpence to see the big giraffe,

"Whiskers on his face and whiskers on his ask your mother for sixpence ..."

We never recited that in front of Mum. She would not have approved.

Dad kept his vow to go swimming every day and, usually, Uncle Frank would go with us. Mum, Aunty Pat and Nan lazed under the umbrella or paddled in the shallows, laughing and splashing each other, letting go of the years as the waves took them back to their youth. I swam between Dad's legs, over and over, until I ran out of puff. Then we threw a ball around with the others, laughing recriminations when someone missed the catch and got splashed in the face.

Barbara, Gerald and his friend Richard disappeared to do the things that teenagers did in those days: meet the locals; hang out at the hamburger shop; check out the girls in bikinis; and then baste themselves in coconut oil so that they would cook evenly and brown on both sides. This always resulted in Barbara and Gerald turning the colour of cooked crayfish with huge bubbles of fluid begging me to pop them. It was such a temptation but I only did it once. I pressed Barbara's shoulder and POP! I'm sure her shriek could be heard back home. Mum expressed her displeasure with a slap around my legs. Barbara milked it for all it was worth, soaking handkerchiefs in cold tea and wearing them on her shoulders like a queen's cape.

One day, we woke to find the weather had turned foul, but Dad had vowed to swim every day and he was "going to get his money's worth." He told me I didn't have to go swimming. It was cold and windy, but I was up for the challenge.

With towels wrapped tightly around our shoulders, we walked through the sand and towards the icy water. We made sure to secure the towels under our shoes so they didn't blow away. Into the waves, we went. Dad dived straight in.

"It's warmer once you get in. Bob down quickly."

I did. He had lied.

It was freezing. As my teeth chattered in the cold, the wind picked up and the waves grew bigger and more frequent. Discretion being the better part of valour, we headed into shore, but as we exited the shallows, Dad froze.

"Grab your stuff," he said. "Quickly."

As we ran, Dad grasped my upper arm – half lifting and half dragging me. Then I saw it. A huge spiral of sand winding its way down the beach and gathering momentum with each yard. The sand felt like a thousand insect bites as Dad lifted me into the remnants of a rickety, old boatshed. He wrapped his arms around me and we huddled on the floorboards with his back towards the wind that seemed to ignore the few boards left on the walls of the shed, bombarding us with sand. The entire structure swayed and rattled and creaked as if it would disintegrate at any moment. I imagined being lifted into the sky like Dorothy in *The Wizard of Oz* and clung onto Dad with my eyes shut tight. As quickly as it had come, the whirlwind left, continuing on its merry way, tossing sand and rubbish bins and everything else in the air. Dad looked at me and laughed. I was covered from head to toe in the sand with only my wide, green eyes showing.

The next day was Christmas Eve and much more relaxing. It involved Uncle Frank and Dad going to the shop to get hamburgers. What a treat. The fish and chip shop in Yarraville only served just that. A hamburger was indeed a delicacy and this one was as big as a bread-and-butter plate.

As I made my way to the outside loo, I heard retching noises and glanced into the laundry/bathroom to see Gerald hunched over the sink with white fluid coming out of his mouth.

"Mum, Mum, Gerald's being sick. Come quick," I shouted. Mum hurried to Gerald who stood up from the sink with a toothbrush in his hand and a big smile on his face. I didn't think he was the least bit funny. Mum laughed and wrapped her arms around me.

"It was a good joke. Don't be cross (though I was). We aren't laughing at you (though they were). You were being a good little sister."

We all trotted off to midnight Mass. Going to Mass then meant Mum and the others would have time to prepare our feast on Christmas morning. The darkened church building was packed to the rafters with carollers raising their voices – telling us to *Come All Ye Faithful* and lifting our spirits out of the grip of a commercial Christmas to a spiritual one. We found our way to a seat at the back of the church and the warm familiarity of community engulfed us. Strangers united in an atmosphere of peace and love to wish each other a very happy Christmas.

The crowd spilled out of the doors and into the street, filled with the love of humanity and the joy of Christmas. The adults set forth to face the task of getting excited children into bed and asleep so that Santa could deposit a few toys at the end of their beds.

I searched the midnight sky in the hope of getting a glimpse of the jolly gentleman in red flying overhead. Dad saw him, but I was not quick enough.

"How will he find me? Will he go to our house?" I asked.

"Don't worry. Santa knows where you are. The sparrows told him," Mum soothed me as she tucked me into the double bed with Nan.

Mum had me convinced that the sparrows reported back to Santa whenever they saw a child misbehaving or when they witnessed good behaviour. I believed that those sparrows were spies and they were everywhere.

I fought the drooping eyelids with all my strength, but eventually, they won.

The presents have long gone from my memory, but the feeling of joy and love still lives in me. Sometimes it leaks out of my eyes when I remember.

With us all living on Dad's wage, there just weren't enough Christmas roast chicken legs or breasts in one chicken to feed our family. We needed two or three, even if Nan assured us that she was happy with the "parson's nose" (the tail end).

The mouthwatering aroma of Christmas lunch filled the kitchen and then seeped through the house –gently roasting chicken, surrounded by browning potatoes, baby carrots and pumpkin, boiled peas and beans (to have both on the plate was another luxury) and stuffing.

Then came the Christmas pudding, soaked in port and smothered in custard with a dollop of cream on top and hidden treasure of sixpences inside. The rest of the port was poured into a punch for the adults.

I've always thought of Christmas as a bit like exam time in the kitchen. Mum, with help from the women in the family, always passed with flying colours.

We all managed to sit around a table, pushed tight together with two card tables. Christmas crackers and paper hats marked our places. The crackers had silly jokes on tiny pieces of paper. Every joke was read and enjoyed, even if they were met with a collective groan at the predictability. Then we had card games or a chance to try out the toys that Santa left.

Dishes done, gifts exchanged, everyone found a quiet spot in front of the TV, on a bed, or on a rug outside under a tree, to sleep off the glorious excesses of overindulgence. Later, Dad decided to go for a walk and I wanted to tag along.

"I'll ask Frank to come, too. We'll ask the locals what the flounder fishing is like here," he said. We looked about the house at the mattresses strewn on the floor but – no Frank.

"Pat, do you know where Frank went?" She had been asleep and did not know. We thought he might have gone to the beach and looked from the end of the street into the sea. Frank was not among the few people bobbing in the water or lying on the sand.

Dad's pace started to quicken. I could feel the tension as he reported back. We all spread out to search for him. Thoughts of swimming, cramps and drownings swirled in our heads.

We took off in every direction, calling out his name.

"If he's not dead, I'll kill him," Aunty Pat mumbled.

One by one, the searchers returned to the lounge room and slumped down. They all looked at each other and shook their heads.

"We'd better call the police."

Aunty Pat let out a wail and the tears flowed. Gerald went to shut the front door.

"Hey, my foot was on that." There was Uncle Frank. He'd been fast asleep in the baby's cot all afternoon.

Aunty Pat held his face in her hands and kissed him over the top of his head and face, covering him with blotchy, red lipstick marks. Then, retrieving the newspaper resting on Frank's stomach, she rolled it up and hit him over the head with it many times before turning on her heel and walking away.

We all laughed except Frank, who looked confused.

"What?" he asked as he tried to get out of the cot with no progress. "Give me a hand, will you?"

No one did.

CHAPTER 9
Let's Party

Mum and Dad loved to entertain, and card parties were a regular occurrence in our house, especially when my cousins, the Mullins clan, came to visit. Two bob [20 cents] in the pot each and the winner takes all at the end of the night. Not much of a fortune, but it was the honour and glory of winning that mattered.

Cousin John was the same age as me and had to endure the ignominy of having to stand back to back at every meeting so that his mother and mine could measure us to find out who was the tallest. John looked so crestfallen when I was deemed to be taller than him. I started to slouch when we were measured, but Mum was onto that trick.

"Stand up straight. Shoulders back." It was very hard on John. The day his growth spurt kicked in, he was deliriously happy.

While the grown-ups played cards, John and I hid under the kitchen table undoing the shoelaces of the unsuspecting family. Distracted by their games of poker or euchre, they didn't notice until home time.

Sometimes, we played pirates in my room – him standing on Nan's bed and me standing on mine, crossing plastic swords or hitting each other with pillows until one of us fell into the crocodile-infested river between the two beds. Our wild imaginations provided a lot of fun times.

When we got to be about 13, we stopped playing imaginary games and played cards in the lounge room.

"Let's play Strip Jack Naked. Whoever loses a game has to take off an item of clothing,' said John with a sparkle in his eye. Sex education at his school was obviously more detailed than at mine. Just then, Mum called, "Supper time," and John was up in a flash. He didn't get supper at his house and the Savoy biscuits with butter, cheese and tomato, sprinkled with salt and pepper, were a big hit with him. Not to mention the jam roll or sweet biscuits. Strip Jack Naked obviously could not compete with supper time.

Mum used to send me to the corner shop to get the biscuits from large tins. The lady behind the counter always asked, "Broken or whole biscuits?" If we had visitors, we got the whole biscuits, but if it was just for us, the cheap, broken ones would do. The lady used to take all the broken ones from each different tin and put them into another one marked "assorted broken" to be sold at half price. Sometimes, if we were lucky, there might even be a chocolate-coated broken one or chipped cream-between in our brown paper bag when we got home. If there was nobody else in the shop to see, that kind lady popped a couple of whole biscuits into my bag – after weighing them, too.

There seemed to be a lot of unplanned parties at our house. Gerald would bring his friends home and they would put on an Elvis Presley or a Buddy Holly record and dance in the lounge room – rockin' and rollin', lifting girls into the air and swinging them about like rag dolls in time to the music. I used to hide behind the couch so I could see the fun without getting in the way.

Barbara, Gerald, Linda, Gerry and me at Gerald's 21st birthday party.

I wasn't completely ignored. One of Gerald's friends, Barry, got a plastic ring out of a bubble gum machine and gave it to me. I thought we were engaged and instantly had a crush on him. He was shyer than Gerald's other more exuberant friends.

When Mum found out Barry wasn't going to have a 21st birthday party, she volunteered to host one, so long as it was OK with his mother. Mum did all the cooking and preparation: sausage rolls, party pies, fairy bread, baby frankfurts, assorted sandwiches and some butterfly cakes that she made especially. Butterfly cakes were little patty pan cakes. The top of the cake mound was cut off and the severed piece was cut in two. Fresh cream was placed on top of the base cake and then the two "wings" were placed into the cream. Simple but delicious. Barry's mother supplied the birthday cake – a fruit cake in the shape of a key.

That night was so much fun. Mum and Dad organised games to play that had everyone laughing raucously. Two players – each with a large balloon carried between their knees – had to walk the length of the lounge room to drop the balloon into a bucket without touching it with their hands. It looked so funny. Everyone watching was squealing with laughter.

Then they were lined up boy-girl-boy-girl in two teams. An orange was pressed under the chin of the first person, and everyone had their hands behind their backs. The orange was passed from person to person, chin to chin, without using their hands – it was so very funny to me from behind the couch. I'm sure the boys and girls quite enjoyed the close quarters, as the orange passed from person to person until the last person held the orange aloft and claimed victory for their team.

Another similar team game involved the outer case of a matchbox placed on the end of the nose, then passed from person to person. Very funny to watch and embarrassing for the participants.

As the night wore on, the girls took off one shoe and put it in the middle of the room. The boys waited in anticipation for the instruction: "Go!" Then all in a scramble, the boys dived onto the shoes and had to find his Cinderella for a slow dance.

Musical chairs were another favourite. There were fewer chairs than participants. The music played; then, when it stopped, everyone had to sit down quickly on any chair. Those left standing were out of the game and a chair or two were taken away. Eventually, the last person seated was the winner.

Gerald entertained with a magic act. He would go outside the door and someone inside would whisper a number between one and five to be "mind read" by "Gerry the Magnificent." Then his partner in crime and best mate, Brian, having heard the number, would sit on a chair in the middle of the room. Gerald would make a big show of placing his hands on Brian's temple to read his mind and Brian would gently clench his teeth over and over, so Gerald could count to the right number and make the big announcement. It was only after a lot of nagging from me that he divulged the secret.

We didn't only have teen parties. We had family parties when all the uncles, aunts and cousins came. That always involved a lot of dancing and music and some of the same games the teens had played. There was a lot of singing and reciting of poems, a dance or two, and someone would play the pianola in the corner of the lounge room, pumping the pedals to belt out a song on one of the rolls that played music.

Late in the night, Mum and Aunty Pat used to disappear and dress in old clothes. They would put a stocking over their faces and a scarf on their heads and then knock on the door. Of course, everyone would turn to see who was coming in, and the sight of the two "rag bag" women hunched over and approaching everyone in the room to get the desired reaction – a fright followed by laughter. Mostly Mum and Aunty Pat's laughter. I think they enjoyed the practical joke more than anyone else.

Dad would play the harmonica or "the spoons" that he clicked together to keep time, while he sang. He had a lovely voice and sang every day – when he wasn't whistling. Everyone was encouraged to have a go, performing their party pieces, and so the proverbial good time was had by all.

New Year's Eve was party time at the Lanes' whether we were at home or a holiday house. The magic of midnight would be heralded in with a countdown, at the top of our voices, in the street out the front of the house. Then followed a raucous

HAPPY NEW YEAR and the banging of pots and pans to make as much noise as possible to wake the neighbours! Then we would join hands in a circle and sing *Auld Lang Syne*:

"Should auld acquaintance be forgot and never brought to mind? Should auld acquaintance be forgot in the days of Auld Lang Syne?" was sung with gusto as a remembrance of those who could not be with us but whose memory was in our hearts.

After that, we would cheer and hug and kiss every person there to wish them a wonderful New Year, and if neighbours were outside, we would go and wish them well for the coming year, whether we knew them or not.

Yes, we had a lot of fun in Yarraville in the '50s and '60s. Thanks to the generosity of my mum and dad, who didn't have much but always shared what they had.

CHAPTER 10
Groovin' on a Sunday Afternoon

The advent of television dramatically changed the Australian culture, as it became a free alternative to going to the movies. The movies on TV might have been very old films, but we watched them on our black and white, 17-inch screens just the same and marvelled at the technology that delivered them into our lounge rooms. Movies, cartoons, cowboys, variety and game shows filled the screens and made local heroes of people such as Graham Kennedy, Pete Smith, Philip Brady and Bob and Dolly Dyer.

Then Australian rock music hit the small screens with *Six O'Clock Rock* and *Sing, Sing, Sing!*, both hosted by Aussie star Johnny O'Keefe.

By the time I was 13 years old, the hormones had started to kick in, so my attention turned to TV shows *Bandstand*, *The Go!! Show* and *Kommotion*. I became obsessed with the bands who performed on these shows.

All girls at St Augustine's Primary School were jumping out of their skins when the church hall was used as a concert venue for rock bands. I was no exception. I was madly in love with Normie Rowe, Bobby and Laurie, Little Stevie Wright and The Easybeats, The Cherokees and, most of all, MPD Ltd.

One Easter, Dad was listening to the radio and heard that local group Ronnie Burns and the Flies were collecting for the Good Friday Children's Hospital Appeal.

"Do you want to go and see Ronnie Burns and the Flies?" Dad asked. "You can get some autographs in that book you got for Christmas."

Dad not only drove me to the intersection where the boys were shaking cans to collect the money but he also pushed me ahead of the crowd to meet Ronnie.

I hung back and only managed a whispered, mousy little "Hello." Dad, on the other hand, had a nice chat with Ronnie, then tossed some hard-earned coins into the collection tin. I walked away with five autographs in my book that day, thanks to Dad. I was a shy 12-year-old, but this was a major turning point in my life.

The Good Friday Appeal had given me the confidence to ask Mum and Dad if I could go to the concerts at Festival Hall on Sunday afternoons, and my life got a whole lot more exciting. The front row was the place to be. Rock bands and singers included Johnny Farnham, Normie Rowe, Little Stevie and The Easybeats, Max Merritt and the Meteors, The Cherokees, Johnny Young, Olivia Newton-John and Pat Carroll, Marcia Jones and the Cookies, Bobby and Laurie and (swoon) MPD Ltd.

"Dad. There's a rock concert at Festival Hall on Sunday and all my friends are going. Can I go?"

"Ask your mother."

"Mum. Dad says I can go to the concert at Festival Hall on Sunday if you say it's all right." I leaned in and looked pleadingly at Mum's face for any indication of an affirmative answer.

"Ask your dad if he's willing to take you and pick you up and then we'll see."

"Dad, Mum says I can go if you take me and pick me up."

"OK. Seeing your mother says it's OK."

That's how it started. It was 1965 and I was a 13-year-old schoolgirl trying to manipulate my parents into letting me spread my wings. I was already 5-foot-8 inches and looked about 18 but had no idea about real boys or the birds and the bees. I was content with being in love with my rock star idols, and they were plenty for me.

The wall of the bedroom I shared with Nan was covered in pictures of The Beatles, a magazine photo of Normie Rowe and one small newspaper photo of my favourite Aussie band – MPD Ltd. The MPD stood for the names of the boys in the band: Mike Brady, Pete Watson and Danny Finley. I was smitten with Danny, the drummer. I saved sixpence off my lunch order by having a lettuce sandwich and dutifully wrote to join their fan club. I was rewarded with a coloured photo for my bedroom gallery. I was member number 37.

By now, Barbara had married Gordon and they had moved into their own place – a sleepout in our backyard.

Nan and I continued to share our room and conversations late at night when I was supposed to be asleep.

The gallery on my wall was growing steadily with each new rock idol obsession. Nan would lay in bed at night, the light from the hallway shining on my pictures, and ask me about who they were and what they sang. Nan became quite a fan. Her favourite song was "that postman one" by The Beatles (*Mr Postman*), and she would whisper from her pillow through the darkness, "Turn up the radio. I can't hear it."

"Shhh. Mum will go crook," I answered, but there was no arguing with an 80-year-old in a shared room.

"I like the look of that Paul. He looks like a nice boy." Then the questions would start. She wanted to know all about him. How old was he? Where did he come from? And the most important question: was he a Catholic?

I had a pocket-sized transistor radio that I listened to under the covers long after I was supposed to be asleep.

I'm sure Mum knew what was going on, but she decided not to interfere. Nan and I were building a precious bond. We were bucking the system together and being rebels ... and Mum let us.

Usually, I went to West Melbourne Stadium, which had recently changed its name to Festival Hall, with my friend Christine. She was from a German family and her mother wanted her to be friends with me to help her fit in. When she invited me to hang over at her house I was astounded that she had her own room and a fluffy doona. I had never seen one before, as we had old army blankets.

Dad drove us to the stadium and parked out the back with the roadies. He waited in the car for the two-hour show to finish, listening to the music and studying the form guide in the *Sporting Globe*, trying to pick a winner for the next week. Then Dad would wait for me to get autographs at the stage door, standing a protective six or seven feet away to the side to make sure I was safe from all that testosterone.

Dad had heard the whole concert from outside the back doors. He listened to us chatter excitedly about the bands and who we were madly in love with and how we would faint if we ever got asked out. We were so naïve but full of hormones and the excitement of the day. Our innocent girlish "if onlys" must have caused him to stifle a laugh or two. I have no doubt he reported back to Mum about all the gushing and giggling.

Money was always tight, but we never went hungry and all needs and some wants would be met by Mum's careful budgeting of Dad's pay envelope from Purvis Glover Engineering in Footscray. Purvis Glover made metal objects and tools like nutcrackers. Dad was an engineer and he often came home and put a piece of newspaper on the table.

"Look at this," he'd say and ruffle his hair with his fingers. Tiny fragments of brass showered the newspaper. Dad laughed. There were no health and safety rules then, and he would come home with cuts, bruises and occasionally some metal in his eye. Mum played nurse and always had a remedy for any problem.

My first brush with my music crushes, MPD Ltd.
Photo: Unknown.

One time, Dad brought home a Christ figure he was making to go on coffins. Mum hit the roof and told him to take it back. He had intended to make a wooden cross to put it on, but she was having none of that.

Dad worked a second job on Saturdays and some Sunday mornings at the Mobil service station at the intersection of Roberts Street, Somerville Road and Geelong Road, West Footscray. His brother George owned it, and sometimes I used to go and fill up the oil bottles and clean the windows of the cars while Dad pumped petrol. I just liked being around Dad and making myself useful. I remember going into Uncle George's office and being confronted with a topless woman smiling from a calendar on the wall. I remember feeling embarrassed that my dad should see that, and Uncle George immediately plummeted in my estimation. That calendar is probably a classic now.

One Saturday, after Dad finished his shift in the garage, he said he had a surprise for me. I looked in his hands expecting to see a bag of Darrell Lea chocolates, but there was only grease and an oily rag in his hands.

"How would you like to watch MPD Ltd rehearsing?"

My heart missed a beat and my eyes popped. My mind raced. Was he teasing me?

"I know their roadie," he said. "Bruce and his dad come into the garage, and they live just over there."

Dad led me across the road to a modest double-fronted brick veneer with a long downward-sloping driveway just across from the petrol pumps. Guitar noises were coming from the garage, and we went inside where we were greeted by Bruce.

"G'day Gerry. This must be Maureen," Bruce said, and I smiled shyly. Looking past Bruce, I saw three young men inside the garage – Danny setting up a drum kit, Pete with a cigarette in one hand as he strummed his guitar with the other and Mike flashing a smile that showcased a mouth full of shiny white teeth.

"Testing one-two," he said into a microphone. They stopped what they were doing and welcomed us. They recognised Dad and said they were glad to have an audience because they were rehearsing a couple of numbers for tomorrow's show at Festival Hall.

I don't remember much of what happened next. I was spellbound. I don't know if it was the music, the excitement or shyness, but I don't think I said a word other than hello and goodbye and perhaps nodded my head when Dad told them I was a big fan. I must have heard the music, but I was consumed with how I looked. I wished Dad had told me. I should have worn my good jeans. But all I could think about was telling my circle of friends on Monday. Nobody at school was going to believe this.

The next day, in the car on the way to Festival Hall, I told Christine all about it and watched her turn green with envy. I think my 13-year-old self was pretty pleased about that. When we got there, we made our way down the front right-hand side of the stage, jostling for a prime position next to the amplifiers. We met some school pals and waited in excited anticipation. I blurted out the events of yesterday, but this was greeted with either scepticism or "I can't hear you," as my voice got lost in the avalanche of screams when the first act appeared.

It was a big line-up because it was the last show before Christmas: Billy Thorpe and the Aztecs, Normie Rowe, Pat Carroll and Olivia Newton-John, The Strangers and Stevie and The Easybeats. What a lineup. But the biggest thrill was to come.

"Put your hands together for MPD Ltd!"

The boys made their way onto the stage and plugged in their guitars. Mike glanced down at the audience. He saw me and flashed those teeth again – I smiled back. He leaned into the microphone.

"This song is for Maureen," he said, motioning to me with the plectrum in his hand. I thought I would faint on the spot. Every girl from my school let out a squeal and pushed in close to me.

"You know him?!"

Drinking in the moment, I stood there, looking at my idols, trying to act cool while a thousand butterflies fluttered in my stomach. A smile lit up my face as I realised that a horde of jealous tweenagers were looking on with envy.

The following Sunday was the fan club Christmas Party at Emerald Lake football field. MPD didn't have a huge following, so they combined with the Easybeats fan club to thank all their admirers with a Christmas Party "meet and greet."

I begged my parents to take me. It wasn't hard to convince Dad because he quite enjoyed his trips to Festival Hall, and now he knew the boys. He also liked catching up with Bruce. Mum was sceptical but packed a picnic lunch.

I was so excited. The hormones were racing. I think I tried on every outfit I had in my meagre wardrobe – twice – eager to look my best. I looked in the mirror and wanted to iron my hair straight, but Mum was having none of that. Curls would have to do.

In December 1964, Emerald Lake was a long way from Yarraville. Few freeways existed then and, like going to Chelsea, it took forever in bumper-to-bumper Sunday traffic.

When we finally got there, most girls were wearing mini-skirts and long, white lace-up boots. They had tinsel in their hair or Santa hats and looked quite festive. I felt embarrassed because I didn't have the uniform. Mum wouldn't let me wear my skirt too short and boots were a definite no-no. I wished I had thought of putting tinsel in my hair.

We had just parked the car and got out when Danny came striding up to say hello to Dad. The men shook hands and talked for a couple of minutes. Danny turned to me and said he was going to see Stevie Wright and asked if I wanted to meet him. So it came to pass that a starstruck 13-year-old was introduced to the famous Stevie Wright. Stevie got a clean skivvy out of his car boot so he could have a photo taken with me! When we stood together, I realised why they called him Little Stevie. He had to reach up to put his arm around my shoulder.

As Danny and I walked back across the field, his voice took on a wistful tone and he began to confide in me.

"It's very difficult with all these underage girls hanging around. I want to be a good role model to the young ones, but it's nice to find someone more my age to talk to," he said. I was 13 and he was closer to 20.

He turned towards me, put his hands gently on my arms and gazed into my adoring eyes. What's happening? Are all my Christmas wishes coming true? He leaned forward – our eyes locked. Yes, yes, he was going to kiss me! My first kiss will be with Danny Finley! At that moment, I was crippled with nerves and stepped backwards ... down a rabbit hole.

Danny tried not to laugh as he helped me up.

My face was so red I couldn't even look at him. He walked me back to the car where I went over and over the wonderful events of that afternoon. But the calamitous rabbit hole incident overshadowed all the exciting things.

I never told Mum and Dad. I don't know if I was more embarrassed that I nearly had my first kiss or that I had so catastrophically messed it up. Either way, it was much too embarrassing to tell my parents.

My nearly first kiss was with Danny Finley. Later my drawings came in handy.

CHAPTER 11
We Love You, Yeah, Yeah, Yeah

In 1964, The Beatles were almost everyone's favourite band, except for the Italian kids and the Rockers, who loved Elvis more. It became a kind of competition between the Rockers and the Mods in Yarraville. This friendly rivalry led to many lengthy discussions on the merits of one performer over another, but no one ever managed to persuade the opposition. Sometimes, there were fisticuffs but not in my circle of friends.

All of Australia was abuzz with news that The Beatles would tour Australia. They were coming to our very own Festival Hall. The excitement at school rose to an unprecedented pitch.

I had no hope of going to see them. The tickets were too expensive for me to save enough money by ordering lettuce sandwiches for lunch. So I did the only thing an obsessed Beatle maniac could do – I entered competitions.

Most competitions involved phoning into the radio station. We didn't have a phone, so I would have had to wait in the phone box, outside the local milk bar, to make a call at the right moment. My entry opportunities, therefore, were limited to write-in competitions.

One was run by Surf washing powder. The competition involved making "a Beatle wig out of an empty box of Surf." That was a bit of a challenge, to say the least. Nevertheless, Mum always used Surf, so I asked her to save the empty box for me.

I had no idea how to go about that task of turning the box into a wig, so I cut it open and flipped the box over. On the underside, I drew a pen portrait of Paul McCartney and sent it with a short story on why I wanted to see The Beatles. I must have been pretty confident because I asked my big brother if he would take me.

"You get the tickets and I will take you," he laughed. He thought he was pretty safe. I didn't have "a hope in hell," according to him.

A few weeks later, I was at school in the back row of the assembled grade reciting a poem for our elocution teacher, Mrs Keats. The girl next to me whispered into my ear.

"I heard your name on the radio. You won tickets to see The Beatles, you lucky duck."

I don't know how I controlled myself, but I looked straight ahead and continued with the poem. My face must have lit up like a Christmas tree because Mrs Keats chastised the girls for talking. The news was spreading through the assembled ranks like wildfire. I remained silent, excited and rather smug. The teacher hit the desk with the ruler to regain the girls' attention.

"Settle down. Settle down. Why aren't you all like Maureen? You can see from her face how much she is involved in this poem!" she thundered.

The big day came. The Beatles had touched down on the tarmac at Melbourne Airport, then located at Essendon, and they were whisked away into limousines for the slow drive through city streets lined with Beatlemaniacs. Mum, Dad, Nan and I all stood on a kerb in anticipation of seeing the slow-moving car grant us a glimpse of the Fab Four.

The distant screams grew closer as the cars headed for the city. By the time they got to where we were waiting, the cavalcade had sped up and whisked by in a blur. I saw a vague outline of what looked like George cramped up against the window. He wasn't looking my way, but I didn't care. I was thrilled to have seen a Beatle.

All the girls were abuzz with varying tales of encounters with the lads from Liverpool. The headmistress, Sister Fara Lambert, marched up and down the narrow aisles between our desks on the warpath.

"Who went to see The Beatles on the weekend?" Her eyes narrowed as they searched the room, her mouth contorted into a miserly smile. I was the only one in the whole room who raised my hand. Her heels stamped on the floorboards as she made her way towards me. Without warning she grabbed my fringe in her fist and punched me in the head three times, pulling my fringe as she did.

"I'd expect that from you, Lane," she growled and turned on her heel and stepped up onto the platform to preach about the evils of modern music.

I don't know who it was but someone got back at her in a big way without her even realising it.

Every morning when the bell rang, we lined up in our grade levels to march into class, standing like soldiers in the playground. Sister Fara, who was not only our teacher but also the principal, addressed our assembly over a microphone with the news of the day. After that, she put a disk on the record player, and we would march to class in formation in time with the music.

Someone had given Sister Fara a new marching record. She was very pleased with her new acquisition, and we all got ready to lead off with our right foot.

Off we went, striding out to the music. But something was amiss. I knew this tune. It was a musical piece called *The Stripper* by David Rose, which featured in movies of exotic and fan dancers. We really got into the marching that morning, swaggering around the playground wriggling our hips and stifling our smiles. Sister Fara was oblivious.

None of the other nuns or parents told Sister Fara what the music was all about. Perhaps everyone was as frightened of her as we were.

The big day arrived. I was going to the Beatles' concert at Festival Hall. My brother, Gerald, was working for a music company called Orchestral in Melbourne's CBD, next to the Regent Theatre. By the time he finished work, he was sick to death of rock and pop music, but he had promised to take me and he always kept his promises.

Mum handed me some money and told me to buy a ticket for the train. I had clear instructions to get off at Flinders Street Station and walk up to The Regent Theatre.

I was very nervous. I'd never been on the train by myself before and certainly didn't know my way around the city.

Fortunately, the travelling went off without a hitch and I was soon at Orchestral, surrounded by records, sheet music and pianos. Gerald gathered his belongings and we made our way across the road to the café. There I was to have a new and exciting experience – a taste sensation called a blue heaven milkshake, compliments of my big brother.

Another new experience awaited me. Gerald had the use of the company van and had parked it in the multi-level car park. I'd never seen such a place – so many floors and so many parking spaces. Nothing had prepared me for the experience of sitting in the front seat as the van swerved around corners, down ramps and around more corners. The roof of the van looked as if it would scrape on the roof of the car park as we went over the humps and bumps.

As we approached the venue in West Melbourne, my big brother said: "You are not to scream. I don't want to be embarrassed in there." I nodded obediently.

The atmosphere in Festival Hall was electric. The support acts were local boy Johnny Chester and New Zealander Johnny Devlin backed by the Phantoms. I'm sure they were wonderful, but I had ears only for The Beatles. I was already formulating stories to tell Nan when I got home and my friends at school.

The tension built to a fever pitch as John, Paul, George and Ringo walked out on the stage. The noise was like nothing I had ever experienced. They were playing and singing, but all I heard was the shrill screams of frantic teenagers jumping up and down, standing on seats and bubbling over with emotion that filled their eyes and dripped down their cheeks.

There was an older woman seated in front of us. She had an umbrella with a handle that she used to hook around the neck of the girl in front of her every time she jumped out of her seat and blocked the view.

I stuck to my promise. I did not scream. I did not stand up. My big brother surveyed the room and saw the assembled masses jumping, dancing, standing and screaming. He looked at his little sister and saw her tears running down her face.

"Oh, go on then, scream!" he yelled, and another voice was added to the throng.

School Days

The whole school talked about nothing but The Beatles, yet Sister Fara decided not to engage in any more conversations on the subject. She chose to pretend pop and rock music didn't exist and go about school business unsullied by the evils of teenage music.

We called her Ferret-Faced Fara or "Fara away the better" – never to her face, of course. Not when she dealt out punishments for misdemeanours such as spelling errors or failures to finish a maths test in a set time.

"Hold out your hand," she would snarl. She would step up onto the platform at the front of the classroom so she would be taller than us. She kept a brown leather strap tucked in the back of her belt under her veil for easy access, ready to strike if anyone put a foot wrong. She called the strap "Flicker." She introduced us to it on our first day in her class, and we saw Flicker just about every day after that. The sting of that strap is indelibly imprinted on my memory – if not my hands.

As part of our homework each night, we would be given 10 words to learn how to spell. We would be tested for accuracy the following morning. I would lie on the floor of the lounge room on my stomach with my knees bent and legs crossed in the air behind me while I rested on my elbows. I would write my spelling words on a piece of paper and get Barbara to test me until I knew them all. Then I completed the rest of my homework while watching TV on the floor in the middle of the carpet.

"I don't know how you can concentrate," Dad would say. Then he'd shake his head and leave me to it. I was good at school work and usually did very well in tests, but the threat of Flicker for each error got the better of me.

After mastering my list of spelling words at night, when the pressure was on the next day, I'd invariably forget at least one. Then the accusations would fly like bullets out of Sister Fara's gritted teeth.

"You can't tell me that you learnt your spelling. Come here and hold out your hand."

Out came Flicker. She would bring it down hard on the palms of my hands or legs. One strap for each mistake.

At 13, I experienced a growth spurt, so Sister Fara had to stand on her tippy toes on that platform to be as tall, if not taller, than me.

Sex education from the nuns was a mystery. We got a diagram of female internal organs and nothing about males. I had no idea what dwelt within male jeans. Boys' bits remained a mystery. We were schooled on the science of our own bodies but not those of the opposite sex. It was all as clear as mud.

The nuns brought in the big guns to explain the slogan "Just say no!" The parish priest sheepishly walked into the classroom and stood next to the chart of female organs. He was supposed to make it all clear.

"If a boy wants you to sit on his knee – don't. If a boy wants you to kiss him and touch his neck – don't. If a boy puts his hand on your knee, slap it away. I think that about covers everything, Sister," said the priest before going on his away. No questions. No clarity. No idea what we were saying "no" to.

As my time at St Augustine's came to an end, I had to think about which secondary school I might attend. There was a choice between St Monica's in Footscray and Mount St Joseph's in Altona.

"You have a decision to make," said Mum, "Mount St Joseph's is a school to go to if you want to be a teacher or a nurse. At St Monica's, you will learn typing and shorthand, cooking and sewing, so you need to consider what you want to do for a job. You also have to think about the uniforms. If you go to Mount St Joseph's, you will need three uniforms: winter, summer and sports uniform. If you go to St Monica's, they have only two uniforms: winter and summer. St Monica's are just the blue and white check, and we can get those from Fred's Emporium in Yarraville. There's a lot to think about. Mount St Joseph's uniforms only come from one shop and are expensive, but your dad and I have thought about it. We can find the money if you really want to go on with your education."

It was 1965 and I was 14. After two years in Sr Fara's grade 7 and 8 with 49 other students, I wanted to get out of school as soon as possible. Another deciding factor was that our rented house at 50 Fehon Street – the only home I had ever known – was to be sold and we had first dibs on buying it, so Mum and Dad were trying to scrape together the deposit.

I didn't want to be the reason we didn't get to buy our house or burden my parents as they tried to make ends meet. So that was a deciding factor, coupled with nagging self-doubt. Academically, I'd been a big fish in a small pond – always in the top two in my grade. I was nervous about going out into the big world at Mt St Joe's and competing with a new mob of kids for the top marks.

The nuns at St Monica's were kind. They didn't hit us or shout. The old nun who was the principal was hunched over and her hands were gnarled and crippled with arthritis. Sr Charles was a very young nun who taught us typing and shorthand. She wasn't that much older than us and was very pretty under her brown and white habit and veil. She sometimes sat on the desk to teach us. That would have been scandalous at St Augustine's, but at St Monica's, nobody seemed to mind.

It was in my first year at St Monica's that the incident of *The Stripper* marching song had a viable contender for the most embarrassing mistake by a nun. Fridays were often a time to finish off projects and work from the previous four days, but on this particular Friday, the principal gathered us all in the hall.

"Sit on the floor, girls, and make yourselves comfortable. We have a real treat for you this afternoon. The maintenance man has brought us a film called *Good Neighbour Sam*, and he is going to run the projector for us to watch it together," she said.

About 20 minutes into the film, we all realised that the title didn't have much to do with being neighbourly. The star, Jack Lemmon, spent the whole movie bed hopping between his wife and his next-door neighbour. The film's screwball plot was harmless enough – he lusts after his neighbour but it all comes to nothing in the end. Yet it was not really suitable for nuns or schoolgirls aged 13–14.

Most of the girls thought it was hilarious and very risqué, but our poor headmistress and the maintenance man were mortified. She hurried up to the projectionist and he slammed off the power switch.

"I'm so sorry, Sister. I didn't know. I'm so, so sorry."

I've never seen a projector banged shut so quickly. I had visions of it being hurtled out of the window into the street or the nuns having an exorcism to rid the hall of all that obscenity.

It brightened up a dull Friday afternoon, that's for sure.

Before too long, I would be leaving behind nuns, marching songs and school. I would be out working in the real world.

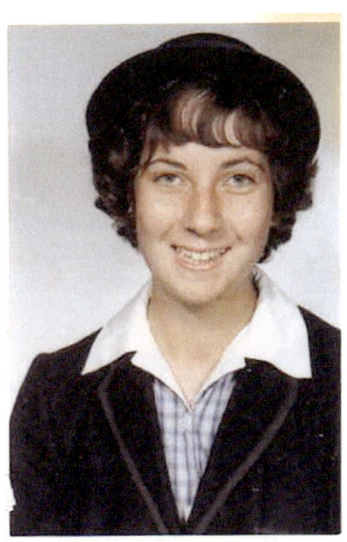

Me ready for St Monica's in Footscray, before I took my first job, aged 14, at K.P. Rees.

Work and Boys

I began work at K.P. Rees Solicitor in Melbourne as a 14-year-old temp, relieving the secretary who was on leave. The principal of St Monica's was a trusted employment agency for some Catholic employers at the time.

Many companies phoned to ask her to fill a job vacancy at their workplaces. When K.P. Rees wanted a temp, the sister asked me to fill in for a stenographer. I must have done a good job answering the phones and doing the filing because, after the two-week stint, they asked me for a repeat performance when another of the secretaries went on leave. I don't recall much about the job except I had to collect the lunch orders, which meant I had to navigate my way around Queen Street and surrounding eateries – quite a challenge for a nearly 15-year-old with little experience of walking alone in the city. I remember they were kind and patient with me.

"Good morning, K.P. Rees office," was how I answered the phone. One time, the voice on the other end asked to be put through to the boss.

"Who's calling, please?" But I couldn't hear the reply. I asked three times and started to get concerned that the man on the other end of the phone might think I was a bit of a dill. Instead, he was very kind.

"Ripper – as in Jack the …," he replied. I laughed and it broke the ice. After that, I smiled whenever he phoned. Another nice, patient man.

The day before I was to say goodbye to K.P. Rees, St Monica's principal called to offer me a job at Mayne Nicholas Transport on Footscray Road. Mum took me for the interview and Dad waited outside in the car.

At that job, I typed the invoices for the Princess of Tasmania – a ferry between Melbourne and Devonport, Tasmania. I also typed the manifests for the Princess – no mean feat. The manifests had to be perfect and no mistakes were allowed, so if I hit the wrong key, I had to put crosses through the whole line and then type it all again – in triplicate.

If goods were delayed, I had to stay back to work overtime on Friday nights. I think they chose me to work because I was paid only $15 a week. If I stayed back until nearly midnight, I got the princely sum of $19 a week plus $5 "tea money."

I didn't mind working late, but it was very scary coming home. The company paid for a cab, but I had to wait at a deserted loading bay for it to arrive and drive me home in the early hours of Saturday morning. The company provided a security man to wait with me, but I was always afraid as the shadows flickered and the silence of the night enveloped us. The security guy just wanted to go home and didn't engage in conversation.

Another thing I disliked was when I had to walk across from my upstairs office to another office via an overhead walkway, which crossed the warehouse floor. All the workmen would try to perve up my dress as I crossed doing "the walk of shame." I held my skirt down in case an errant gust of wind caught it and gave the eager eyes a glimpse of my white Cottontails knickers.

Wolf whistles were commonplace. I always had mixed feelings about them. On one hand, I was quite flattered that I was considered reasonably good-looking. On the other hand, I didn't like being lusted after. Not that I knew anything about what it was they were after. I was still sadly ignorant about sex.

One of the jockeys on the trucks was Fred. The jockeys helped drivers load and unload the trucks and kept the drivers company while doing deliveries.

Me aged 15 with Fred.

I met Fred in the cafeteria. I was bending over the ice cream fridge, reaching for a Peter's Drumstick when he spoke to me. We chatted for a few minutes, with an audience of prying eyes from the canteen. He asked me to go to the movies (a big drawcard), but I had to tell him there was a proviso – he would need to ask my parents.

Fred had to come to the house and meet my family before I was allowed to go anywhere with him. Dad gave him the third degree, asking about his job and prospects. Mum asked about family and religion. He must have passed because we went to the city to see a movie.

Fred was 16, English and had a Beatle haircut. To my just-turned-15-year-old self, that was a big plus. I had never met an English person before and he had an accent – not exactly like The Beatles but close enough. He had recently moved from Southall in Middlesex and had no friends in Australia.

"I left all my mates from school back home," he said. I was drawn to the exotic background and felt sorry for him being alone in a new country.

Going out with Fred turned out to be a huge mistake. We were way too young and had very little in common. He was lonely and devoted all his time to pursuing me. Eventually, he expected all my time, and I became cut off from my other friends.

When I met his parents, they were polite but uninterested in me. They lived in a rented house near Seddon Station. Fred had a sleepout in the backyard. We went into the sleepout to listen to records and kiss. I still knew nothing about sex.

I was so naïve; it was over before I even knew it was starting. I asked him what he just did. "We just made love," he said. I said, "That can't be right. There must be more to it than that." He assured me, "No. That was it."

I was confused, embarrassed, upset and very angry at myself for allowing that to happen. I wished I had known what was going on. All my Catholic upbringing whooshed over me like a tidal wave. I cried.

In my muddled 15-year-old mind, I was convinced we were married. We had done the deed and there was no going back – in the eyes of God, we must be married. Sister Fara's words hung in my ears, "No one would ever want a girl who has lost her virginity." I believed her.

Fred and I went out every weekend and got to know each other better. Fred could be fun and we did like the same music. We went to see The Who, The Animals and The Hollies and had a good time.

However, Fred also had a bad temper and would dig his nails into my hand if I said anything with which he disagreed. I felt trapped but continued with the relationship. I was torn between feeling sorry for him, grateful to him for taking me out so much and resentful and wishing there was a way out. But it was too late. We had done the deed. There was nothing I could do.

My parents didn't like him and he knew it. Even Nan, who liked everyone, told me I should find someone else.

Fred was aware of their opinion, though it was never mentioned to him. He started to hatch a plan.

Fred was very persuasive. "Let's run away together. Your family is going to break us up if we stay here. We'll go to Adelaide. There are lots of English people there."

It was then that I committed the worst sin of my life – something I have never forgiven myself for doing. We ran away from home and went by train to Adelaide.

At the time, it didn't seem real. It was an adventure – a scene in a movie. Just like the little girl acting out a movie plot in the backyard at home, I acted out a scene from a romance. With one foot on the platform, I was sure something would happen to stop us going, and I kept looking over my shoulder. Unfortunately, nothing did go wrong and we set up a house at the foot of the Adelaide Hills.

I can't explain why I did such a terrible thing to my parents. When I look back, I feel ashamed, but I also feel as if I was someone else – not me. We were so young that we weren't anywhere near mature enough to make the choice we did.

What started as an adventure turned into a nightmare. We "played house" in Adelaide and our money ran out quickly. We tried to find work, but that was difficult. I went for an interview to clean motel rooms and the owner interviewed me at a table. I glanced down to see his erect penis standing at attention, out of his pants. I left quickly. That was my first experience of being the target of a predator, and it was very scary. We needed the money, so Fred wanted me to take the job anyway and made up some excuses for the man.

"He's probably harmless. Maybe he didn't realise," Fred said. But I wasn't going to go back.

We lived on a tin of soup and a small loaf of bread a day. I was miserable but didn't know what to do. Then Fred got a job and made some English friends who took us under their wings. They invited us to parties and picnics, and we even went to a nightclub to see The Twilights play. Fred flirted with a girl called Mary at a basement club. I felt humiliated in front of our new friends and blocked everything out except the music and the band.

Just before their last set, the drummer came to our table and asked me if I would like to go to a party after the show. I was flattered but declined.

The Swinging '60s were not a thing I lived through really. There was no swinging for me. It's not part of my persona to cheat. I can't say the same for Fred.

One of our new friends, Trevor, was interested in what we were doing so far from home and we told him what we had done.

"You have to go back. You have to let your parents know you are OK," he urged.

Thankfully, his wiser head prevailed. He talked us into going home and drove us in his Mini Minor all the way from Adelaide to Yarraville, so neither of us could chicken out.

It was a long trip – eight hours with only toilet and food stops. I didn't eat anything. I was sick all the way – worried about confronting my parents. I vomited a couple of times.

Not knowing what I would find, I tentatively walked through the door at Fehon Street, to be greeted by tears and loving arms. Then a lot of questions. I was still only 15, so there was talk of involving police and carnal knowledge charges. I don't remember what happened next; it's all a blur. What I do remember was how thin Mum had gotten. I was consumed with regret and guilt for having caused my family so much grief. That guilt has never left me. They had been grieving my loss as though I was dead. It broke my heart to have been so stupid, selfish and thoughtless.

CHAPTER 13
'Til Death Do Us Part

Arrangements were made for a wedding.
"You don't have to marry him, you know," Mum said. "You are not the first and you won't be the last girl to be taken advantage of."
I heard the words but didn't believe them. I felt like I had to marry him. I had to make this awful thing I had done right.
A few weeks before the wedding date, I was panicking and resolved to call it off – to try to go on with my normal teenage life, even though my reputation was in tatters. The evening I made that decision, disaster struck.
Fred had just left my house to make his way home on his bicycle when he was hit by a car. Unconscious, he was rushed to the hospital. When he woke, his eyes were permanently damaged and he had a turn in one of them. He had to look sideways to see straight. This made him very self-conscious. While he was lying in the hospital bed, he was frantic, "This won't affect us, will it?" What could I say? I was trapped.
We married three days after my 17th birthday on August 24, 1968.
The wedding was at Our Lady's in Altona, and the reception was at our neighbour's house across the road. Mum did most of the catering, ordering bakery goods from the cake shop.
Fred's friend from Adelaide, Bodgie, came to be the best man, and his girlfriend, Tess, was my bridesmaid. I had no friends to call on. I was just embarrassed about the whole thing. That feeling increased 100-fold when Fred and Bodgie flicked cream from the cakes at each other during the speeches. We were too young to be married.
After the wedding, we went to Adelaide for our honeymoon weekend. We caught the train and spent time with Bodgie and his new girlfriend. Tess was no longer in the picture. She just came to the wedding with him because I didn't know the new girl.
Back in Melbourne, we moved into a flat in Cowper Street, Footscray, and joined the youth club and tennis club at St Monica's Church. That was great fun. We went out with kids our age who were footloose and fancy-free and from good families. I made some good friends.
I started working at The Alfred Hospital and loved my job. I worked in the typing pool and delivered mail etc. to all the wards. I knew a lot of people and gathered a new group of friends around me at work. The lunches were great. The chef made his own bread rolls that were deliciously warm at morning tea time when I had mine with butter and Vegemite.
It was hard to work all day and then cook and clean a flat at night, but that wasn't the worst thing about marriage. Fred and I didn't get along. We argued about money a lot of the time. He liked having a bet on the races and kept control of the money.

I shopped and cooked but had very little money for myself – just what I could save from the grocery money. Our arguments usually ended in violence. I was too embarrassed to tell anyone. My family had their suspicions, although they never mentioned it. We were both too immature for the pressures and responsibilities of married life.

Four months after we wed, I found out I was pregnant. Fred was angry at me, but I didn't know why. I didn't know anything about contraception. Apparently, I was supposed to "take care of that."

When Deb was born, Fred held my hand, and his early disappointment turned to joy. From the moment the nurse placed little Deborah in my arms, I knew my life would finally have meaning. I had no idea how to be a mother, and I was very nervous, but I knew this kind of nurturing was my destiny.

The most precious things in my life came from my marriage to Fred: our two beautiful daughters, Deborah, born just a couple of weeks before our first anniversary, and Jeanette, who arrived two years later. They were the light of my life, and I devoted myself to them.

While I was pregnant, Mum and Dad moved to Surfers Paradise in Queensland. Dad's brother, George, had bought a new garage and offered Dad a job. They sold the house on Fehon Street and moved into a flat on the Gold Coast. Mum and Dad drove down to see me after I had the baby. They were both thrilled to hold little Deborah in their arms. They loved the lifestyle up north but missed us kids and their grandchildren too much. Eventually, they moved back to Melbourne, paying to have a granny flat built behind Barbara and Gordon's family home in Hanna Court, Braybrook. I was glad to have them home.

Little Shop of Horrors

In 1971, Fred got a payout from the car accident he had on his bicycle – a little windfall that could have set us up in our own home. I wanted to buy a house in Footscray, but he wanted to be "his own boss," so we bought a milk bar in Somers Parade, Altona.

By this time, I was pregnant with Jeanette and could hardly fit behind the counter. Deb was two years old and into the lolly counter whenever my back was turned. Fred had access to the money in the till and would disappear to play cards behind the butcher's shop a few doors up from the milk bar. Once he even went to the races without telling me.

I was very shy and had to learn to interact with people quickly, so the shop was good for me in that respect. The milk bar helped me to become more outgoing and gave me the confidence to talk to people. I tried to be friendly and obliging, even during the 3.30pm crush when the kids would get out of school and head to the milk bar for 20 cents worth of mixed lollies. I would crouch down behind the glass cabinet as the children lined up with their coins in hand.

"One of those, and two of those, a musk stick and two Clinkers, a packet of Whizz Fizz. No wait, put the Clinkers back. I want four liquorice blocks and one Clinker …" and so it went on. Ten to 20 more kids waited with money in their hot little hands, while adults paced, impatiently, wanting to buy smokes or milk.

I always tried to treat the kids with the same respect I would give to adults. I resisted the urge to roll my eyes or tell them to "hurry up," but the daily ritual at the lolly counter tested my patience occasionally – especially when the child would spend what seemed like an eternity choosing just the right combination of mixed lollies to then say, "Put them all back, I want to start again."

"You'll have to work out what you want and wait until I serve all the adults who have been waiting for you. Next time, try to make sure you know what you want."

Fred opened the shop at 6.30am and manned the counter until I had fed and taken care of the children. Then, around 9.30am, I would take over for much of the day.

Jeanette was born and we were both happy to have that little bundle of joy join the family. But the day after she arrived, in the hospital, I became sad and weepy. They call it post-natal depression now, but it didn't have a name back then. I didn't want to go home to the milk bar.

The day came and Fred collected us from the hospital. I went into our house behind the shop, each step heavier than the last, to feed my baby girl. Deb was excited and very gentle with Jeanette, patting her hair gently and holding her little hand.

"Look, Mummy, she likes me," Deb grinned.

I had barely finished feeding Jeanette when Fred called from the shop: "Come and help me."

I had not had time to rest after leaving the hospital. All I wanted to do was have time with my babies, but I needed to serve customers. I resented it so much that this incident, which was nothing to Fred, became a "resentment rock" for me to carry.

Life in the milk bar was very stressful. Jeanette was a good baby, but I was still helping run the milk bar during the day and looking after my family in between customers. I was still only 20 years old.

We were open from 6.30am to 9pm or even 10 o'clock on hot summer nights. Sometimes, bikers would park their motorcycles outside the front doors, come in for cigarettes or milkshakes and just hang around the front of the shop, scaring the locals away.

Some younger kids used to jump the fence behind the milk bar and get into our yard, where they would pinch glass bottles, then bring them around to the front of the shop to sell them back to us for five cents each. We knew they were doing it but didn't want the confrontation.

One time, Fred confronted a group of youths on push bikes and asked them to move along and allow other people into the shop. Instead, they stayed outside the shop long after we had closed, flicking lit matches through the air vents at the front of the shop. Thankfully, the matches died out before reaching the floor and didn't start a fire. I never found out why they did that. It seemed like an overreaction.

I remember my 21st birthday was a happy time spent in the back of the shop after closing time at 9pm. We played cards with Anne and Lorraine, our part-time, schoolgirl employees. They took the pressure off me when I was a new mother and, at 17, they weren't much younger than I was. George Scharenberg, who was a family friend and lead guitarist with the band Patchwork Quilt, came too, and we all played a game called Donkey that made everyone laugh uncontrollably. There may have been some wine involved.

Lorraine and Anne became my friends and confidantes, and I looked forward to seeing them come through the door after they finished school. Once, I even managed to get away from the shop to go to Altona beach. It was a hot summer day and the girls were asleep at the back of the shop where Fred was serving. Lorraine, Anne and I dived into the water wearing our T-shirts and jeans and emerged from the sea with our T-shirts and jeans clinging to us like Ursula Andress in a James Bond movie. We laughed and laughed some more. I felt quite the rebel. That day was a feather I carry, and I smile at the memory now, wondering if Lorraine and Anne still remember the occasion.

Our small business didn't withstand the amount of "outgoings" from the till, and we were going broke. We put the shop on the market to avoid bankruptcy. It was a very trying time. The stress was incredible, but we found a buyer and moved out without a backward glance.

We moved into a rented flat in Oxford Street, Newport, where Deborah started kinder. I helped out as treasurer of the Mothers' Club. Fred got a job working for a plastic bag factory and quite enjoyed the work. He stayed on in that industry, later building up his own business from which he made a lot of money.

One day, at a working bee at the Oxford Street Kindergarten, one of the dads rolled up on a motorbike along with some biker friends.

"They look a bit rough around the edges," remarked one of the mums. Nobody wanted to talk to them. They were working hard in the hot sun, so I took a tray of cordial drinks out to them. One member of the group was David King. I didn't know then, but our paths were destined to cross many times.

Back to Yarraville

It was 1973 and life in the flat on Oxford Street was difficult. It was hard to keep my growing girls quiet so as not to disturb the neighbours, and, worse than that, my underwear and other clothes kept disappearing off the shared clothesline. I was unnerved by the thought of my underwear being in the possession of some scary individual. I started to feel as if I was being watched but dismissed it as imagination.

One hot summer night, Deb was in her cot and Jeanette was in a bassinet beside the double bed. Fred was asleep near the open window. I lay awake next to him, listening to my little ones' gentle breaths and trying to sleep.

In the darkness, I heard a noise. Not much. Just something that made me open my eyes. The curtain had been moving in the air that cooled the room, but now there was a man's leg straddling the window. For a second, I didn't believe what I was seeing. Then I let out a scream and pushed Fred hard with two hands towards the window. The intruder scampered out of the window and ran along the balcony and then down the stairs.

Fred chased him to the foot of the stairs, where the intruder jumped on a bicycle and rode away. I comforted my babies and tried to settle myself. We resolved that night we would find somewhere else to live.

We moved into a rented house behind the second-hand bookstore on Anderson Street, Yarraville. I was back in my hometown and just around the corner from Mum's sister Dorrie and brother-in-law Dan Heffernan.

Uncle Dan worked in the office at Luna Park in St Kilda. Sometimes, he got free tickets for rides like the Big Dipper rollercoaster or the Fun House with its crazy mirrors. He had lived his early life on the edge of the law and told exciting stories about the old days when, as a child, he had "kept nit" (been a lookout) for Squizzy Taylor – a notorious criminal who became a bit of a legend in Melbourne's Depression era.

Uncle Dan was always very dapper in his grey suit and hat and must have been quite a ladies' man in his day.

Aunty Dorrie was Dan's mental equal, but she was physically disabled and housebound. She walked with the aid of a stick, seldom leaving the house for fear of having a fall.

I called to see her every day with Jeanette while Deb was at school. I would go up the street to get groceries for her, and she would look after Jeanette while I was shopping. Aunty Dorrie would give me the money in an envelope with her list written on the outside. On one occasion, I realised how long it had been since she had gone to the shops. Aunty Dorrie sent me to the grocery store with instructions:

"Get me 20 cents worth of soup vegetables." When I placed the order, the proprietor laughed out loud and handed me a carrot. Later, I went back to Aunty Dorrie and explained about inflation.

Uncle Dan bought a new car. Instead of trading in his EH Holden for a pittance, he gave it to me as thanks for doing odd jobs, shopping and chores. I had my very own car. I was so excited. I had the freedom to put the kids in the car and go, wherever I chose, without the hindrance of bus timetables.

I strapped the girls into booster seats and sang at the top of my voice. I could see Deb through the rear vision mirror with her fingers in her ears, but it did not deter me. I resolved that my children should be treated to show tunes like those from *Jesus Christ Superstar*, *Man of La Mancha* and *Godspell*. That last one might have been a mistake because Deb grabbed its showstopper – *Day By Day* – with both hands and sang the one line, "Day by day, day by day, day by day ....," over and over, never getting to the next line. *Puff the Magic Dragon* got the same treatment, "Puff the magic draggy, Puff the magic draggy," from little Jeanette.

During this time, Fred had started managing a local rock group called Sweet and Heavy. The boys spent a lot of time at our house. They were fun. It was good to see their enthusiasm and have music filling the rooms. They were a pretty good band and Fred managed to get them a gig on *Hey, Hey It's Saturday*, an enormously popular weekend TV variety program.

I took the kids along to the studio to see it being recorded. There was no studio audience and the girls and I had to sit over to the side. They were wide-eyed in anticipation of seeing the hosts Daryl and Ossie. Ossie was a puppet ostrich, operated by Ernie Carroll, whose jokes were often risqué but went over the heads of the kids watching. The show worked on different levels, and come Saturday morning, all age groups were glued to Channel 9.

When Daryl Somers arrived, he came straight over to the kids to talk to them. They beamed at him, but little Jeanette was overawed and hid behind me. While we were chatting, singer and Australian star Johnny Farnham came into the studio. He excused himself for interrupting and Daryl introduced me to him. He was gracious but was in a hurry to organise plans for later, so they walked off towards the studio door, deep in conversation. I sat there with my heart pounding and smile beaming. I was thrilled. Memories of Festival Hall and hero-worshipping flooded back. I settled back into my chair to enjoy the taping of the show.

"Shhh. No talking, Jeanette. Keep watching. Ossie is coming soon," I whispered in the darkness of the almost empty studio. She was getting restless. Then she saw Ernie Carroll reach into a suitcase and pull out Ossie Ostrich, shoving his hand up its rear end.

"That's not the real Ossie," she complained over and over, frowning accusingly at me. "That's only a puppet. Not the REAL one." She stuck out her bottom lip and glared at me as if I had gotten her there under false pretences.

They started filming and Jeanette was still complaining over and over, "That's not the real one." There was another character on the show, a squeaky voice called Angel. So when my little angel was complaining loudly, Daryl heard her and spoke into the microphone.

"I think I can hear the Angel coming ... Oh no. It's not the Angel." How embarrassing.

Fred used to accompany Sweet and Heavy to their gigs and stayed out at venues late into the night and early morning. I spent more and more time alone with the kids. They were my life. I played with them, and we made our own free fun. In the middle of winter, we played a "day at the beach" in the lounge room, with a beach umbrella and towels on the floor and a picnic lunch. Then we went into the bath for pretend swimming.

Sometimes, we lined up the kitchen chairs, one after the other, and played "bus driver" or "aeroplane pilot." Sometimes, we built a cubby house under the table. I enjoyed motherhood. I love my girls more than anything in life.

Sweet and Heavy got a gig at Hastings Hotel past Frankston, on the Mornington Peninsula. They were offered free accommodation overnight and asked me to come along. It was to be the first time I had left my girls since they were born. Although I was excited about the possibility of a little holiday away at the beach, I wasn't keen to leave my kids home with just anyone.

The day came and I kissed my girls goodbye. There may have been tears, but I hid them well. I knew they would be fine with Aunty Dorrie and Uncle Dan.

As soon as we got to Hastings, I went for a walk along the deserted beach. The huddled seagulls, sheltering from the wind, didn't give me a second glance.

The grey sky hung low on the horizon as the waves crashed on the sand and retreated into the bosom of the next wave. More seagulls warily separated, making way for me as I left my lone footprints in the pristine sand. This was the very first time since Deb was born that I had been anywhere on my own. I was totally without another person to take care of or tell me what to do. Much as I loved Deb and Jeanette, as I turned to look back on those footmarks, I realised that at that very moment, for the first time in five years, I was not responsible for anyone. I hugged myself and turned round and round and round. While those seagulls took flight, so did my spirits.

Hastings Pub was full of drunken locals yelling over their beer, "Sing a John Denver song. Sing *Country Road*." Sweet and Heavy didn't do that kind of music, but they accommodated the drunks in the audience as best they could. The song got faster and faster, practically galloping at the end. The crowd grew more appreciative with each amber ale and the mood was friendly. The band members were happy to keep playing as long as they were served cask wine and beer. The sets got shorter to accommodate the drinking time. I decided to call it a night and made my way upstairs.

We had all been given single rooms. I got my key from the desk and found my room. It was a tiny space like a nun's cell, with a single bed covered by a blue,

Sweet and Heavy were lots of fun and spent a lot of time at our house.

George Scharenberg with Deb when he lived with us.

chenille bedspread and a bedside table.

I hadn't packed a nightie. I snuggled into the bed, enjoying the feel of the crisp, white sheets on my skin and the glorious solitude. I had never slept alone before – I had slept with my sister, my nan, then my husband and my kids but never alone.

Almost as soon as the chenille bedspread was pulled up around my neck, I felt the effects of the free Coolabah wine and I needed the loo. It was way down the corridor on the right. I knew I was the only person on the upstairs floor and so, rather than go to the trouble of getting dressed, I wrapped myself in the bedspread and walked through the door towards the communal bathroom.

"Clunk." The bedspread had caught on the door and dragged it shut. There I stood outside the doorway, unable to move, naked under the bedspread that was stuck fast in the door … and I still needed to pee.

"Help! Can someone help me please?" I must have sounded pathetic and looked worse. I don't know how long I stood there, but eventually, a young couple walked up the stairs and stood in bemused astonishment at the sight.

"Could you get the manager, please? I'm stuck." They walked back downstairs stifling a laugh.

The manager came with the master key and set my bedding free of the door. I made it to the toilet in the nick of time. It must have been a comical sight. I'm sure that young couple dined off that story for a month after they got home – spreading the laughs at my expense.

Fred managed another band for a short time – Patchwork Quilt – and the lead guitarist, George Scharenberg, whom I mentioned earlier, lived with us for a while. He then moved in with his girlfriend and later to Whyalla in South Australia. I was sorry when he moved out. He was good company, the kids loved him, and I enjoyed hearing the dulcet tones of his guitar coming from the spare room at the back of the house in Yarraville.

Around this time, late in 1976, we bought a Housing Commission (government housing) new build – a three-bedroom, one-bathroom, concrete house in West Sunshine – and Jeanette started school the following year.

CHAPTER 15
Independence

When Deb was at school and Jeanette was in kinder, I enrolled in a painting class at Footscray Community Arts Centre, where I learnt from Pino Calati. He was quite a famous Italian painter and sculptor. I loved going to class and applied myself to learn all I could from the master.

Eventually, Pino said to me, "I have taught you all I can. You now have to create your own style. I can't help with that."

I gained more than skill in that class – I gained confidence. I started to believe I could paint.

As an 11-year-old, I had sat with my big brother, Gerald, at Mum's red Formica table, the kind made popular in Australian kitchens in the '50s and '60s. It was my mother's pride and joy. I watched Gerald sketch Italian actress Gina Lollobrigida. He gave me a pencil and paper and showed me how to use shading to make three-dimensional drawings. In the 1980s, Pino helped me apply that knowledge to paint.

Gerald had already introduced me to his favourite artists, theatre and music – in fact, all things creative. He is definitely the talented one in the family. He can turn his hand to anything and do it well. Armed with the experience he gave me and Pino's invaluable knowledge, I offered my services to the teachers at my kids' school – St Paul's in West Sunshine. I volunteered to show the children in grade 2 how to draw. I wanted to pass on a love of art to them as my big brother had done for me.

Seeing the children's enthusiasm for my art class was a light bulb moment: I was good at teaching, and I loved sharing my skills. A plan began to formulate in the back of my mind.

We had settled into the Commission house, and both the girls were in school when I saw an advertisement for a teachers' aide at Christ the King Primary School in Braybrook – just a short distance from home. I applied for the job and got it.

My role was to assist the prep teacher, Muriel, with her 43 students. I was paid until lunchtime, but I stayed all day because I couldn't leave her with so many children. I loved being there. We became really good friends and I formed friendships with most of the staff.

The prep-grade children always made me laugh, but their teacher, Muriel, relayed a story of what happened to her that made me laugh the hardest.

"The children were dropping the F-word in the schoolyard," Muriel said.

"The principal complained that I should address it straight away. So, I got the kids together, seated on the mat, and told them that they couldn't say 'fuck' because it's the magic word. That they were not allowed to say the magic word at school or they would get into big trouble," she said.

"I thought that was the end of that and the playground swearing had stopped. A few weeks later, a magician came to do some magic tricks in the classroom, and he was saying 'Sim Sala Bim!' as he waved his magic wand to entertain the children. After saying that five or six times, he asked the kids, 'You all know the magic word, don't you?' They shot each other sideways glances and nodded. 'When I count to three, I want you to shout the magic word as loud as you can.' And they did." Muriel ended the story and we laughed.

I loved going to work at the school. The children were so funny, especially when they got the words wrong. "Our Father, whose aunt's in Heaven ..." comes to mind.

Another funny moment was when a little boy asked: "Do you have a lover?"

I replied: "What do you mean?"

He said: "You know – to lub out your mistakes with." He meant a rubber (eraser). I bit my lip so he wouldn't see me laughing.

The arguments at home had worsened. I used to pray on the way home that Fred would not be there, hoping for some peace for a little while.

On the same block as the primary school was a girls' secondary school. Working in the mornings at the primary school, I was offered afternoons at the secondary school. I jumped at the opportunity and loved every minute of it. My duties included assisting the deputy principal with administration tasks, teaching art and media studies to year 7 and 8 students, and taking students on excursions, with the help of qualified teachers. I was more of a technical teacher, which meant I was still paid teachers' aide pay.

On one excursion, I took some year 8 girls on a bus to Footscray Technical School to use its media equipment. As we travelled along Maidstone Street, one of my not-so-little darlings put her head out the bus window and shouted obscenities at a teenage boy who was walking along the street. He yelled something back and they both laughed.

I closed the bus window and told her I was not tolerating that kind of behaviour and that it brought our school into disrepute.

"Meet me at lunchtime to pick up the papers [dropped in the schoolyard]," I told her. I wanted her to remember that actions had consequences so she would not swear and hang out of the window again.

"Are you going to put me on report, Miss?"

"No, Karen. Just see me at lunch and we will pick up papers and that will be the end of it."

"OK, Miss. Thank you."

Karen was a bit of a rough diamond, and I was a bit surprised when she turned up. We walked around the yard picking up rubbish together and talking.

"When you use language like that in public, people have a poor opinion of you," I told Karen. "They also have a poor opinion of our school and it's not fair to the rest of us if you do that."

"Yeees, Miss," she sighed. Her words agreed, but her tone implied she was just placating me.

She was a tough cookie. At one stage, we had a flasher at the gate of the schoolyard. Karen and her little gang saw him expose himself and ran after him, intent on harassing him. They chased him down the street and he jumped on a bus to escape their wrath.

Not long after that Karen left school and got a job. One day, she turned up at the staffroom door with a big smile and a huge, "Hello, Miss."

We exchanged pleasantries and had a bit of a catch-up. Then Karen said, "Hey, Miss, do you remember when you made me pick up papers for swearing?"

"Of course, I do," I smiled. Maybe I had made a difference to this young girl's manners. I started to feel a bit smug.

"I remember, Miss. You know, every time I swear, I think of you." There was not a bit of irony in her voice, but I laughed out loud.

"I'm not sure I'm happy about that, Karen," I said. Then the penny dropped and we both laughed.

Spot the teacher's aide? Me with Brian's grade at a Christ the King Primary School excursion having fun at the zoo.

Working as a teacher and being paid as an aide was fun. The staff enjoyed each other's company and many socialised outside school hours. Financially, however, it was unrewarding.

Going to work was an escape for me and a real joy. I used to dread going home because the tension in our house was becoming unbearable. Eventually, we decided to end the marriage. Fred moved out and I applied for a divorce.

Being Catholic, that was a big decision, but I needed a clean break. I wanted to apply for an annulment from the church. I couldn't believe the God of love and compassion would want me to stay in that marriage. But first, I had to apply to be legally divorced, so a Decree Absolute was granted.

It was a good decision, and I think we tolerated each other much better after we ended the marriage.

I don't regret marrying so young because I have two wonderful daughters. They are a blessing and I'm truly grateful for them.

CHAPTER 16
My Three Amigos

Joan Smith (nee Carstairs) was the librarian at CTK school, and she and I developed a wonderful friendship. Most people were afraid of Joan. She could be prickly. She didn't suffer fools gladly or otherwise. I don't know why she liked me. I was a bit of a mouse, and she couldn't abide mousey people but still, we got along like a house on fire.

"I can't stand most people. They are boring. You're not boring," she said to me. I thought I was pretty boring compared to her. She had an amazing life that she would recount little by little over coffee or after movies.

Christ the King and my three amigos in 1980. Brian, seated middle, Barry, third row, far left, Joan, second row, far right, and me with a perm, standing centre.

Joan and two other teachers, Brian and Barry, were very supportive of me during that very difficult and tumultuous time in my marriage. I am very grateful to have had them in my life. I had been apart from my old school friends for so long, we had lost touch, but now I had new pals to socialise with and confide in.

Barry, Brian and I became the three amigos, having dinner together and going to a movie or the theatre.

Brian shared my passion for old movies and loved *Casablanca* almost as much as I did. We could both recite most of the lines as we watched the flickering screen, in admiration of a wonderful story, brilliantly acted. He was great company. We would go out for a late meal or a coffee after the movie, but it became a bit of a joke when he left his wallet at home and couldn't pay for his ticket or his supper at the Pancake Parlour.

"Oh, I'm so embarrassed," he would say, apologising, but that didn't stop him from doing it again. We teased him mercilessly.

Brian was a bit of a Lothario. All the mothers loved him and wanted their children in his class, not just for his wonderful teaching skills. He was single and a bit of a flirt.

Barry and I got on very well. He invited me to dinner as his "plus one" many times. He loved a party and was a great cook and a perfect host.

One Queen's Birthday Weekend, Barry had a fancy dress party where everyone was to come dressed as a queen. I was the only woman there.

There were some fantastic costumes, the food was great, the music good to dance to and everyone had a great time. I dressed as Cleopatra with a long black wig and lots of glam makeup. A very handsome, dusky-faced gentleman danced with me all night. We had a great time until I got overheated and took off my wig. When he realised that I wasn't a man, he lost interest immediately and found someone else.

Barry and I would also see Melbourne Theatre Company productions. I would park at his place in Fitzroy, and we would catch the tram into the city. We would have dinner at a cafe or pub before the show and afterwards have a coffee. I would drive home.

Barry, a Bulldogs supporter, Dad and me, North supporters. Photo: Deborah Gough.

On one occasion, I didn't like the show very much and wasn't feeling well, so I left Barry at the interval and went to catch a tram. It was about 9pm, but there were few people around as it was midweek in the city.

While I waited at the tram stop, a man approached me. He jiggled his hands in his pockets and started to talk to me. I moved further up the tram stop. He followed. He started talking about masturbation and it became obvious that he was doing just that. I looked around hoping to see some other people in the vicinity, but there was no one. My heart began to race, and I kept turning my back on him in a bid to discourage him. Relief came when the tram finally arrived, but I was petrified he would get on the tram. Then I would be trapped in the carriage alone with him. Fortunately, as I jumped on board, he stayed at the stop.

"I'm going to think about you in bed tonight," he yelled. My skin crawled and I was very shaken.

Running from the tram stop in Fitzroy to my car parked at Barry's, I trembled as I fumbled for my keys. Scrambling into the driver's seat, I burst out crying. It was the first time I had walked alone in Melbourne at night. I would never do that again.

It was not the only time a man felt entitled to sexualise or put his hands on me. Once I was at the movies in Yarraville and felt something on the seat as I sat down in the darkened theatre. I put my hand down the back of the chair and grabbed hold of a man's hand. I twisted his fingers as hard as I could, and he moved away in the darkness.

Another time, I was waiting in a queue to get onto a plane when the man behind me cupped his hand around my bottom. I got a fright and stepped backwards. My stiletto heel went right into the top of his foot. He kept his distance after that.

At the football with my daughter one day, a drunk squeezed past my seat. Carrying a beer in one hand, he grabbed my breast with his other hand. I was very embarrassed. I couldn't think why he would do such a thing. I was a mother sitting with her child at the footy and he had a disgusting sense of entitlement. I am still sorry I didn't call security, but then, as I looked along the row, I noticed that he was with four or five other drunks and I was too afraid of the potential consequences.

Another sexual assault occurred when my car was making a strange sound. I pulled into the same petrol station I used all the time. I was on friendly terms with the man who ran it. He found a tree twig had got caught under the chassis.

"Thank you. I really should have looked at that myself. I'm very grateful that it's nothing serious. How much do I owe you?" I asked.

He said, "Don't worry about it. Just be nice to me," and reached to stroke my breast. I pulled back, got in my car and never went back there again. I felt quite upset. I couldn't understand. This was someone I knew, and he had made me feel afraid and dirty.

Joan and Ricci

The kids were older now and liked to stay at Barbara's house to play with her daughter, Julie. Barbara was and is a great cook and babysitter. On one occasion, when the girls came back from Barbara's house, Jeanette complained:

"Why don't we have Aunty Barbara's ham on our sandwiches?"

I phoned Barb to find out what the amazing, delicious ham was that she gave my girls, only to be told it was Strasburg sausage with tomato sauce.

School librarian Joan became the most influential person in a turbulent and difficult time in my life. She was my friend, mentor and confidante. I was proud to be her pal.

Joan was quite a private person and didn't usually socialise with the others at school, but she came to my Halloween fancy dress party with her foster son, Ricci. Of course,

Me as Mae West with Ricci at the Tallintyre Road, West Sunshine, Halloween party.

Joan would not dress up. She wore the same pull-on pants, blouse and runners, with a headband, that she wore every day. The headband was to tame her unruly, long brown hair. It hung down to her waist when it wasn't in a bun behind her neck. Ricci was the complete opposite of Joan. He came dressed as a mummy in a costume made from torn, white sheets. His costume was spectacular, and he stayed in character from the moment he cast a shadow over my door.

I was building a fence near the front door. A trench had been dug, so Ricci, always keen to play a practical joke, lay in that trench, in the pitch-black night, waiting for unsuspecting guests to arrive. As the guests made their way up the path in the darkness, Ricci would groan until they looked around suspiciously. Then he sat up slowly, pointing a bandaged finger at them and groaning loudly. It frightened the life out of them. Some ran to the door, while others jumped and laughed before trying, in vain, to engage the mummy in conversation. He was in character and would remain silent, except for the groaning.

That was a fun night. All the teachers came, and we walked down to the shop in costume and had fish and chips for dinner.

I loved teaching and being part of the school staff. A glimmer of an idea began to hatch in my mind. I started to wonder if I might go back to school to become a fully qualified teacher rather than work as a kind of trade teacher on half pay. I found out that I could apply as a mature-age student even though I didn't have an academic record to show them.

"You are the kind of student we want. You have some experience to bring to the tasks," the teachers' college told me.

I spoke to my girls.

"I have something to ask you. I love teaching and I really want to go to teachers' college and learn how to be a real teacher. It won't be easy. We would all have to make some changes and watch our pennies. I would be studying at night, so I would need you to support me in this. I want you to think about it and let me know because this is something that affects you, and I won't do it if you don't want me to."

Deb and Jeanette said that they didn't want me to do it, so I said, "OK," even though I was disappointed.

The next day they came to me.

"We have thought about it. You never stop us from doing anything we really want to do, so we won't stand in the way of what you really want to do." I've never been so proud of my girls. They showed such maturity and empathy in that moment. I was so very proud of the women they were becoming.

Joan encouraged me to go to teachers' college. She said, "Teaching needs more interesting people like you."

Interesting? Me? Not compared to Joan. She was, and remains, the most remarkable woman I have met. She was strong, compassionate, entertaining, funny and kind. She could also be judgmental, quick to anger, selfish and harsh, but none of those things set her apart from the rest of us. What made Joan so remarkable was her personal integrity.

She was a woman before her time. She never pretended to be anything other than what she was – a strong, determined environmental warrior and champion of the oppressed. Her sexual orientation was nobody's business. She always did what she believed to be right and fought against injustice.

Joan's childhood home was at 67 Napier Street, Essendon. Her mother didn't approve of her free spirit and they clashed constantly in childhood and well into adult life. She was a tomboy, although she hated that term. It reeked of gender bias, she said, and was used as a derogatory term. She said this in the late '70s before those terms became commonplace.

Joan felt closer to her father, James Carstairs, who played football for Carlton's seconds in the Victorian Football League (VFL) and played kick-to-kick with young Joan. She loved playing footy and running around with her toy plane. Unfortunately, it flew onto the roof of the neighbour's house. She was climbing up to get it when the neighbours stopped her. They were worried she would fall, but Joan was very confident and could climb just about any tree or structure. She wasn't worried and could not understand their concern. Her brother had been on the roof many times. The neighbours called her mother and Joan was not allowed to retrieve her plane, so it stayed on the roof for about 40 years. Each time she drove by as an adult, Joan would look for it. She was still resentful that she was not allowed to go up there and get it because she was a girl. Every time we drove by she was tempted to shimmy her middle-aged body up the drainpipe to retrieve it.

Joan loved planes and flying. As a child, she would go to the Essendon Aerodrome and watch the planes come and go. She would yell at the pilots, "Hey mister, will you take me up in that?" and many times they did. She said there was nothing as exciting as going up in a plane.

Never one to hang around the house, she would have breakfast or grab an apple and run out the door to play. She would be gone until dinner time. She put her climbing skill to good use, scrambling up the neighbours' fruit trees to get the best pieces from the treetops. She always had a pocket full of coffee beans, which she ate like lollies. I remember the wide-eyed look of delight on her face when I presented her with a packet of chocolate-coated coffee beans. They became a staple of her diet.

As a teenager, Joan loved riding on two wheels and hung out with a gang of girls who all rode motorbikes. She loved the wind on her face and the excitement of speed. She also rode a pushbike everywhere as a child as well as later in life. She lost a pinkie toe when her foot slipped while wearing thongs and her toe went through the spokes. After that, she wore runners everywhere.

Joan's wild streak didn't prevent her from getting a good education – first at Essendon Primary and then at Essendon High School, but when she left school there were not many choices available to women. There were only two career options open to an educated girl – teacher or nurse. She chose to teach.

During the last year of her teacher training, she taught at Monivae, a small rural area just outside Hamilton in Victoria. She was yet to be fully qualified but had to teach in a kind of apprentice capacity, although she was responsible for the whole school and had a visit only occasionally from the school inspector, who reminded her she was not fully qualified. The school had only one room and her students ranged from 5–14 years of age. Joan was only about 17.

Joan's favourite lesson was sport and she played footy with the kids – boys and girls were encouraged to play. But her sporting passion was cricket. She took pride in being a member of the first female cricket team at Donex Cricket Club in Essendon. She would also lecture all and sundry on the origins of overarm bowling because "women invented overarm bowling when their crinolines got in the way of their underarm bowling," which was what the men had done in Victorian times. Men adopted the style that women had invented.

Her relationship with her mother remained strained. On return from her country teaching appointment, she decided to marry Bill Smith. She got married so she could move out of home but said Bill was nice enough. He played country footy and was a good man.

Together they had a baby boy, Tony. But Joan was not cut out for married life and regretted the move. She preferred the company of women and didn't know what to do with a baby. She told me she was afraid she would break him. She gave Tony to her mother to raise.

Joan continued with her teaching career. At one stage, she went to teach at Eslanda School, Morley, WA. Many of her students were from poorer socio-economic backgrounds and had special needs. Some were Indigenous children and she had a soft spot in her heart for them. She was always helping out families with legal issues or even with grocery money. It was here that she met Heather, one of the school mums. They formed a special bond and became great friends.

Heather had been separated from her husband and had in Joan's words, "a tribe of kids." Heather had a dalliance with a famous Aboriginal footballer, from Perth, who played in the VFL in the 1960s. When her husband came back to her, Heather was pregnant with the footballer's child. The husband wanted to take care of his family but not the new baby. Heather had baby Ricci in the hospital and Joan visited her to make sure all was well.

"I was so worried about what I was going to do with this little baby," Heather later told me.

"I went home but I couldn't take him with me, so I left him in the hospital and went to visit him every day. I thought I could talk my husband around (into accepting the baby), but I couldn't. I used to see Joan at school all the time. I knew she was a good person but, one day, when I came to visit Ricci, I heard someone singing in his room. I just hung back a bit and watched. There was Joan with Ricci in her arms, singing to him. She was looking at him in a way that I just knew she should take him and look after him until I could get my husband to change his mind. So, I asked her to take him, and she did," she said.

Joan had Ricci for 19 years. With Heather's permission, Joan moved back to Victoria and brought Ricci up there. She sent Heather fare money so she could visit Ricci. Heather always sent cards, phoned and kept in touch. Ricci, Joan and Heather had a bond that endured the test of time. The physical distance did not affect the relationship.

Joan had friends from all walks of life. She had a group she called her "witchy friends": a group of same-sex-attracted women who gathered together to drink and socialise. Joan didn't drink alcohol. She made fun of the silliness that ensued at those meetings. I asked her if they were real witches and she said they were "white witches" and only interested in love spells. Joan did, however, produce some white powder for Deborah's tinea. She said it was a potion she mixed up, but I suspect she bought it from the chemist. She liked to play her little jokes on naïve me.

In Western Australia, Joan became friends with Rolf Harris's wife, Alwen Hughes, for whom she had a lot of respect. She also knew the Australian wife of Hollywood actor Vincent Price, Coral Browne.

In the 1970s, she became friendly with the famous Junie Morosi and politician Jim Cairns. All of them were pictured on the front pages of newspapers, arms linked, in the front row of the anti-Vietnam War protests.

After this photograph was published, she was called into the principal's office at the Catholic school in Braybrook.

"Are you a communist?" the principal asked.

Joan proceeded to give her opinions on a variety of subjects, including religion, ideologies, communism, Catholicism and basic morality. I think the principal was happy with her responses but happier still when she left the room. Joan had a poster on her classroom/office door that read: "Everyone is entitled to MY opinion." She lived by that. She also had a mischievous streak. After the discussion in the principal's office, Joan wore a Maoist cap with a red star on the front to work, even though she was not a communist. She liked to stir the pot.

CHAPTER 17
Friend and Mentor

Joan and I began our friendship over morning tea and coffee in the staffroom. We bonded over a love of old movies, and she introduced me to her favourites at Carlton Movie House on Saturday nights. She loved Greta Garbo, Marlene Dietrich, Ingrid Bergman and Maureen O'Hara. We watched so many films there that I can't remember them all, but I will mention a few: *Queen Christina*, *Anna Karenina*, a double feature of *The Maltese Falcon* (Myrna Loy) and *Casablanca* (Ingrid Bergman), *The Black Dahlia*, *Salt of the Earth* and *Celine and Julie Go Boating*. The last one I loathed. Two women in a boat, with subtitles. The plot has a death and the scene gets repeated over and over with slight twists and discoveries. I got thoroughly sick of it and could only groan: "Oh no, not again." I just wanted to know who did the murder so I could get out of there. Joan was enthralled by it and loved every minute. Meanwhile, the cola I had consumed was making life uncomfortable. I sneaked out to

A self-portrait of Joan who changed my life and influenced me from the moment I met her.

the loo. When I got back, the movie was finished. I never did find out who did the murder. I didn't even care to ask.

After the movies, we would go into Genevieve's, the cafe next door, have coffee and cake, and talk about the films. The cafe had a toilet at the back of the room and, inside the ladies, there was a small hole in the plaster with an eye drawn around it. Someone had written over the top, "Here's lookin' at you, kid." We laughed and laughed. Joan bought me a graffiti book and we had a good laugh at that. I miss the days when graffiti was clever, appropriate, entertaining and funny. Now it's just racist or tags.

We also had a similar sense of humour, which came to the fore when Joan took

Gypsy lady or Gina Lollobrigida. Joan behind the camera.

a lot of photos at a staff night out. Most of the staff had a lot of fun, fuelled by a fair amount of alcohol. She blew up the photos and put them on the staff room wall with space to add captions. Oh boy, did that cause a lot of fun. Eventually, the comments became so rude and funny that she had to take them down. It was such a fun time.

One St Patrick's Day, Joan put green food dye in the tea urn and turned the sugar green. Some people got a bit cranky, so she decided to needle them a bit more by posting a sign in the staff room: "Beware the Ides of March." We plotted for a week to play pranks on the staff – a little bit of harmless fun. We put plastic spiders in the sugar and a wooden leg in the fridge. I blacked out my front teeth with paper. We strung a washing line across the nun's desk and pegged Tighty Whities men's underpants on the line. There were so many little booby traps, I can't remember them all. Everyone was either confused or laughing by morning tea time. Nobody laughed more than Joan and me.

Sometimes, the principal would ask Joan to get some lunch meat for the tuckshop and she would ask if she could take me. I was only part-time, so I was probably not getting paid for the time worked anyway. I don't think the principal could win a fight with Joan, so he always said yes. Of course, Joan's wicked sense of fun would kick in. We would be off on a magical mystery tour to get meat from Gilbertson's in Altona rather than the local supermarket. She liked to escape, as she put it.

I was teaching art and craft lessons to the whole school by then, and art lessons were always well resourced after a visit with Joan to the Reverse Garbage Truck in Carlton. It was not a truck but a big old warehouse filled with garbage bags of factory offcuts. We found everything from material, rubber and leather to metal filings, tiles and coffin handles at different times. Joan would avoid the 10 o'clock "ethnic hour," as she called it when the members of the local Italian community would pick through and take all the best bits. They would get quite aggressive with each other over a good piece of cloth or lace. We had to get there early for prime pickings.

On the way there, I commented on the name "Hygienic Lily" on a building. We laughed. It was a factory that made paper cups and plates, but Joan said it sounded like a call girl had set up a business. Her wicked sense of fun kicked in and she took

Joan and I had many laughs and imagined an elaborate story for "Hygenic Lily".

a photo of me in my sexiest dress (which wasn't that sexy). She developed it with the title Hygienic Lily. That photo stayed mounted on the wall at her home until long after her death.

I suppose that people suspected that we were a couple, but that was never the case. When someone mentioned it to me, I was surprised. I had never thought of our friendship being misconstrued. I loved Joan, but I was never that way inclined. She was more my mother's vintage than mine. We were best friends – it never crossed my mind that we might be the subject of gossip. Not that it would matter. Joan's sexuality wasn't anyone's business, not even mine.

Joan was a rock for me when Fred and I decided we would stop pretending and end our marriage. It was tough to be a woman alone but tougher still to be in a loveless marriage.

A year later, I was going through divorce proceedings when Ricci began visiting to see if I needed any odd jobs done and to mow the lawn. He moved most of the rocks out of my yard and did some general gardening work, too. We would talk and sit on the back verandah, drinking cordial and eating biscuits and cheese. I assumed Joan sent him.

I told Joan how grateful I was to him and commented that he must *really* like gardening. She said she couldn't get him to push a mower at home. It wasn't gardening he liked; it was me. I thought that was very sweet and rather flattering.

Pubs, Punts and Pastures

Joan had a big influence on my girls, especially on Deborah. It was Joan who put the thought into her head of becoming a journalist. From that day, Deb worked towards her goal. She was successful in that endeavour for 35 years, before starting her own writing and publishing business.

Jeanette was a little afraid of Joan. She didn't like children who hovered, and Jeanette was always close to me. Joan would tell her to go and play, but she wanted to hang out with me and stayed at my elbow. Joan could never understand any child wanting to be around adults. She had never wanted to be around her mother.

The school staffroom was where our book – *Pubs, Punts and Pastures* – was conceived. Joan was talking about her family heritage and she asked about mine.

With a puffed-up chest, I jokingly told her: "My family was Footscray's aristocracy. My great-grandmother was the first white child born in Footscray."

Joan replied: "What was her mother's name?"

Without thinking, I blurted out "Mrs Pickett." It was like a red rag to a bull for Joan: "You don't know her name?"

Then and there, Joan decided to educate me in the ways of the Public Records Office in Cherry Lane, Laverton. We were to spend many days, months and years poring over old documents that were tied in red tape. She showed me how to use the microfiche reader. We found Margaret Dowd Pickett, and my great, great-grandmother had a name. From there, we pieced together our book.

Joan was researching three women from Keilor while I was discovering all about Margaret Dowd Pickett and her sister, Ann Dowd Delaney Harrison, their half-brother, Michael Lynch, and their niece, Maria Kilmartin. It was like finding pieces of a jigsaw puzzle. Sometimes they didn't fit, so we would have to revisit what we thought we knew, add new information and discover a different narrative.

All this Joan typed up on the computer. I wrote mine longhand because I didn't have a computer. Joan copied it onto our manuscript and proofread everything.

I would call or visit my relatives and ask them what they knew about our ancestors. When I ran out of the family that I knew, I took to the phone book to see if I could find others. It was a great joy to discover new information – a bit like Sherlock Holmes solving a mystery. We got to know the women in our manuscript very well. We felt as if we had discovered them and gave them life in the pages we wrote. We acknowledged those six ordinary women in that time and place and brought them into the 20th century. We helped them live in human memory again.

Researching at the Public Records Office and the library to find gold nuggets of history was exciting. Hours and hours of diligent sorting through dusty, literal red tape to find a piece of the puzzle created a great partnership between Joan and me. It enhanced our friendship. Nobody else understood the excitement of uncovering a fragment of the past as we did. It was a shared interest at a time when we were both in need of a distraction. It was a lot of fun.

As the stories in our book grew, so did our excitement about what we were uncovering. We realised that ordinary women were intrinsically interesting and had extraordinary tales to tell because nobody had told them before.

Joan was a member of the St Albans History Society. We asked if they would finance the printing of our manuscript if we repaid them with money from the sales of the book. They agreed, and we set about making our stories look like a book. It took about 18 months.

In 1988, our *Pubs, Punts and Pastures – A History of Pioneer Women on the Saltwater River* was launched by Mary Delahunty, an award-winning ABC TV journalist, at Footscray Community Arts Centre on the banks of the Saltwater (Maribyrnong) River. She would go on to become a Victorian MP and a minister with the portfolios of education, planning, arts and women's affairs.

It was an apt location, as this was where my ancestors had lived and worked. I took a back seat at the launch – Joan gave the speeches and stood in the limelight. She was very good at getting publicity and never seemed to get nervous. I was glad to let her do all that. The downside was that I was sometimes forgotten, but never by Joan. She always said we would never have started the project if I hadn't told her about Mrs Pickett. Of course, I would never have had the confidence or skill to research and write it without her. She had the experience and skill and taught me everything I know about research.

Joan was quite worried that we might not cover the printing costs and end up having to pay back some of the money to the history society. She needn't have worried. The book sold out of the first 1000 copies and went to a second run. Eventually, those 1000 copies sold and it was out of print. We paid back the society and then had to decide what we would do with the rest of the money.

Neither of us wanted to keep the proceeds. It didn't seem right. We wanted to have some physical manifestation of the lives of the women from our telling of their story – something that would keep them in people's minds long after the book was gone.

The Pubs, Punts and Pastures book launch with Joan and Mary Delahunty.

Joan had the idea of asking the Living Museum of the West whether they would call for designs to create what she called "a hut on the Maribyrnong." Museum curator Peter Haffenden was keen to be involved and set about making it happen.

Writing *Pubs Punts and Pastures* was intrinsically

rewarding. We saw our project as extremely important. We took our roles seriously, as ordinary women in history were seldom documented and, in time, their stories were lost. We tried to make a difference with our humble book. We wanted to inspire others to write women's stories and to value the narratives from the maternal lines of their families. We wanted to let the women in our book speak as loudly as men had traditionally done. We hoped that our efforts would prompt others to listen to the women in their homes and write their personal histories, thereby valuing women's work in and out of the home. We wanted women to be valued.

The cover of Pubs, Punts and Pastures.

The book had an unexpected consequence. It created a new bond between Mum, Joan and me and helped me feel closer to Nan and her story, even though she was no longer with us. We all learnt things we didn't know about each other, as well as about the women in history. In the process, I was trusted with family secrets from the distant past and also from the lives of my mother and grandmother. Through their memories, I got to know them as women – not just as mothers and grandmothers.

As a consequence of acknowledging the role of ordinary women in history and valuing their contributions to Footscray and Victoria, we opened the door for other historians to re-examine how they approached research, so they began to include women's stories.

Although out of print for many years, a PDF of the book can be downloaded for free from the Pubs, Punts and Pastures Facebook page. A second hardcopy reprint was due for release and sale in 2024.

Accolades for Pubs, Punts and Pastures

The following is an extract from a Living Museum of the West brochure (1997) to publicise our book and the rotunda that we financed with the proceeds.

"Authors Maureen Lane and Joan Carstairs who wrote a book, Pubs, Punts and Pastures, about early women pioneers in the western suburbs, said, we found 'that much of the actual work of settlement was done by a lot of women whose husbands, conveniently or inconveniently, died young. They left young

widows with large families and acres of fairly barren, very dry, stony land to complete the job alone that had been started by a 'husband and wife team.'

The book looks at the lives of six women, all related and connected in ways. A number of these women were part of the history of this west bank of the Maribyrnong River that gave birth to Footscray. Margaret Pickett kept a herd of dairy cows on the banks of the Maribyrnong near Footscray Park and ran the Ship Inn and the punt in front of it.

A few short years later in the early 1850s, Margaret's sister, Anne Delaney, came to the area and they ran a punt together further upriver where Lynch's Bridge is now, right near the Flemington Racecourse. In 1853, Anne Delaney bought the land where the Footscray Community Arts Centre now stands. In 1873, she sold the land to Henderson, who established the ham and bacon curing works, known as "The Piggery."

In 1854, Anne built the Junction Hotel on the corner of Bunbury Street and Whitehall Street, and after that, she built The Rising Sun Hotel.

The family has left its mark with local street names, such as Pickett Street, Ann Street, Margaret Street, Joseph Street, Cuthbert Street and Catherine Street in Footscray.

Joan Carstairs and Maureen Lane painstakingly researched the lives of these women. Their research tells stories that would otherwise be lost in time. Anne Dowd came from Ireland at age 22 in 1849 with her husband and young son and gave birth to her baby daughter on the ship at sea. The family ran the Punt Inn and operated the punt. Eventually, they bought land of their own. When her husband died and Anne remarried, her land became the property of her new husband – as that was English law. They built, and she ran, the Rising Sun hotel in Footscray. After her second husband died, Anne was arrested for cursing in public and sent to gaol when she discovered that he had spent all of their savings and slowly sold off all of her land to enable his status as a gentleman. She outlived all of her children and died a pauper in Geelong Gaol at age 75."

Joan Carstairs and me at the rotunda that was built with the proceeds from Pubs, Punts and Pastures. The rotunda can be found at Pipemakers Park, Maribyrnong, near the Living Museum of the West.

Blowin' in the Wind

Like his father, Ricci had become a very good footballer but he had no interest in school. He loved art and had a wonderfully comic way of presenting his artwork. Joan would always have his paintings and drawings on the walls, and she framed her favourites.

Ricci was no stranger to hard work, but once he had mastered a skill, he wanted to move on to something else. He had a string of jobs. He was always very popular in the workplace but would tire of the job and just stop going. Money was not an issue. He never valued it. He would leave a job with money owing to him and not give it a thought. Then Ricci met Anita, a Jardwadjali girl with a huge smile and orange curls, from the Gippsland area in northwest Victoria. They fell in love and conceived a child together. Ricci was 18 and Anita was 19.

The couple lived with Joan in her St Albans home and she supported them. I remember driving with her and being stopped by charity collectors at the traffic lights. The guy shook the tin at Joan, and she asked for which charity was he collecting. He said for an Aboriginal welfare centre.

"I've got my own," Joan replied and drove off.

Ricci and Anita had a baby boy and called him Tony, after Joan's other son. Ricci's biological mother, Heather, was thrilled to be a grandma. Ricci decided to take his little family to Western Australia to meet his other mother.

The living conditions at Heather's were very different from what they were used to in Melbourne. There was no food in the house for the kids who lived there, let alone baby Tony. Ricci went to the local supermarket when it was closed. He was filling a trolley with food when the police arrived. He was arrested and placed in detention at a centre surrounded by razor wire.

Joan maintained that, if he had been white, he would have been out on bail. Instead, he was incarcerated. Joan expected to have to send money to pay a fine or bail, but that request never came. It was one of many "if he was white" statements Joan, and later I, would make.

What happened next was beyond horrific. Nobody knew why Ricci tried to escape. There was a theory that the heavy prisoners in the remand centre had threatened him. He was a very handsome boy, and he might have been assaulted. Joan thought Ricci might have tried to escape simply because someone said it couldn't be done. He liked a challenge.

We never found out why he climbed on the razor wire where he got stuck. What we do know is that a guard shot him in the head while he was snagged on that wire. He fell back and hit his head on the concrete. It was 1982.

Ricci was in a coma when the police came to Heather's house to tell her he was in the hospital. She asked what had happened and they laughed and said, "The usual." They left Heather to find her own way to the hospital in the middle of the night. If she had been white, they might have driven her – it would be "usual" to give a mother a ride to the hospital. Heather thought Ricci had been raped. She was upset when she called the cab. The driver refused to take her unless she paid first. Again, if she had been white...

From the hospital room, Heather tried to contact Joan but she was at school. When Joan arrived home after work, she discovered that all the lights were on. She thought Ricci was back from WA.

"Ricci?"

There was no answer. She called out again. In his room, she found all his artwork had come off the walls and was lying on the floor. Then her phone rang.

Joan was devastated by the news. We sat in the staffroom the next day while she told me what had happened. She wanted to rush over there, but Ricci was not expected to live through the night, so she didn't go. The next day, Ricci was still in hospital. Joan told me she felt as if he was waiting for her to get there. She asked if I would take care of her cat while she was gone. She left on the next plane to WA. Ricci died just before she got to his room.

Joan went into warrior mode. She demanded that the government take responsibility for his burial. She didn't want Ricci to be buried with no marker, like some of the women in our book. She wanted a proper grave for her boy. She argued that if he had been permanently injured, the government would pay for his treatment, so they should pay for his funeral seeing as it was their employee who had fired the shots that had killed him. It was the very least they could do.

It was a hard-fought battle, which she eventually won. Ricci was buried while Bob Dylan's *Blowin' in the Wind* played, and his two mothers clasped each other for strength.

The injustice of the whole thing prompted me to go to every newspaper – including the local papers. I wanted to tell the world that Ricci had lost his life for the sake of a few groceries. That a boy of 18 could be executed for not staying where they put him. They had not yet convicted him of any crime. I wanted to shine a light on the injustice of putting a young Aboriginal man in remand for attempting to steal food. He should have been out on bail like any white boy caught stealing food.

No one was interested and one journalist said, "That's a Western Australian problem, not ours."

Joan was to keep fighting to get some justice for Ricci. She was instrumental in having his death included in the Royal Commission into Aboriginal Deaths in Custody. She also assisted a filmmaker in creating a short film about Ricci called *A Little Life*. Joan had asked Ricci how he was going to support himself as he got older. He answered that he didn't expect to have a long life. He was going to have only a little life.

Ricci and Joan with two other teachers at our famous fancy dress party.

Back home, Joan was lying in bed trying to sleep when she heard the wind chimes on the covered verandah. Her first thought was "Ricci is coming through the window again." Then the realisation hit her. He was gone. The next day, she said she felt Ricci had let her know he was "alright" with the movement of the chimes.

Joan had a relationship with Chrissie, an artist and mother of three children. The family moved into Joan's house for a time. I remember phoning Joan and hearing Chrissie yell "It's your friend!" Joan came to the phone and called me by name as she took the phone. I asked how she knew which friend it was. Joan told me she only had one person she called her friend. She had pals, lovers and mates, but I was her only real friend.

After Chrissie and Joan went their separate ways, she lived alone for much of the time and embarked on other history society projects. She took others under her wing and wrote or co-authored other publications. I visited regularly. She would always be happy to show me what she was working on. She was also pleased to meet my grandson, Conor. She said she didn't like little boys, but this one was not too bad.

Not long after that, Joan had a stroke, which affected her walking. She tackled this with her typical strength and determination.

When frustration crept in, she would get a bit grumpy or short-tempered. I would tell her to stop grumbling.

"You're the only one I let put me in my place," she would laugh.

I continued to visit Joan every few weeks. I had graduated from teachers' college and was working as a prep teacher in Altona Meadows and then at Sunshine. When I visited, she would growl at me for not visiting more often. By then, her son, Tony, was living with her. He took care of her needs, but she missed our coffees and chats.

I was shocked when Joan passed away. I thought she would go on forever. She was such a strong personality and a wonderful friend. I couldn't imagine being without her.

Joan was a spiritual person but not a religious one. She believed in an afterlife. She said it would be arrogant to think we know everything and how it all works. She told me in her afterlife she would inhabit a cockatoo; she loved them and always wanted to fly. The day after her funeral, a lone cockie flew over my house squawking loudly. I always thought that was probably Joan sending me a message that she was alright, just as Ricci had.

SHORT FILM - A LITTLE LIFE

The story of young Aboriginal Ricci Vicenti who died after being shot while attempting to escape from a remand prison. The film was initiated as one of the FTI Stipend Scheme projects and has now been completed. The film is quite an extraordinary review of one person's life and its impact on others.

Vicenti was adopted at the age of six months and travelled through Europe with his foster mother. He lived for some years in Melbourne and then returned to Perth.

The film features interviews with both of his mothers along with drawings, paintings and Super 8 footage that Vicenti shot during his little life. It is expected to be released nationally later this year before being broadcast on television. Produced with the support of the Film and Television Institute of WA.

Source: The Film and Television Institute (WA).

CHAPTER 19
The Getting of Wisdom

I looked down at my hands in my lap. They were shaking uncontrollably. I clutched them tightly so nobody would notice my nervous tremors as I waited in an office in Ascot Vale. A panel of Mercy Teachers' College academics were about to interview me.
"You left school at 15?"
"Yes, I had to go to work to help out my family."
"How were your grades?"
"I was always in the top two in my class."
"Ah, but this will be very different – much more difficult. How do you think you would cope with writing assignments?"
I reached into my bag and produced *Pubs, Punts and Pastures*. I placed it on their desk:
"I don't think I will have a problem with that."
The man in the middle of the interview trio reached forward to pick up my book. He turned it over in his hands. The whole tone of the interview swung 180 degrees. Their stern faces started to crack into smiles and raised eyebrows. The remainder of the interview was about my book – questions I could easily answer. I heaved a sigh of relief as I made my way to the door. As I left the office, I was floating on air.
I didn't have to wait for a letter in the mail. I knew I had a place at Mercy. They told me on the spot:
"We think you will be an asset to education."
I had to miss the orientation weekend at the Melbourne University campus because I couldn't ask anyone to take care of my children for a whole weekend. I didn't want to be away from them for that long anyway. With no orientation to guide me, I was a bundle of nerves on my first day of classes. My hands shook so much. The first time I wrote my name at the top of an assessment paper, I couldn't recognise my handwriting.
My first tutorial was philosophy: J. S. Mill.
"Oh, my goodness. I'm out of my depth and drowning in philosophy," I screamed on the inside, while I slumped in my seat at the back of the auditorium. I went home deflated and insecure.
That night, I picked myself up out of my slump. I tackled the problem with Mill in one hand and a writing pad and pencil in the other. I painstakingly transcribed each paragraph of that book into understandable English. It was a mammoth task. When my fellow students found out, they offered to buy it from me. We were all struggling with Mill.
The exam was nerve-racking, but I did very well – thanks to my translation into everyday language. I understood the questions and, more importantly, had answers that were informed by experience as well as the text.

Teachers' college wasn't all hard work. I got to do a painting every week and loved every minute of it. The lessons I had from Pino at the Footscray Community Arts Centre stood me in good stead. I had also taught art to the kids at school, so I was quite confident in that class. I was a prolific painter. When we had an exhibition of our artwork in the foyer, I had as many paintings on display as all the other students in my class combined. When Mum and Dad attended the opening of the exhibition, they walked into the foyer and my art teacher looked at Dad.

"I know that face," he said to Dad, who looked at him quizzically. Then the lecturer indicated to Dad's portrait, which hung in pride of place in the exhibition.

Dad stood tall as he looked at his image on the wall and tears welled in his eyes.

"I'm very proud of you, you know," he whispered.

In art class, I met Kriss Oliver. We had only a cursory friendship in college, but it blossomed when we began working together. She became my lifelong sister of the heart.

Jenny has been a constant from my uni days to today and David, the love of my life.

In sociology classes, I was paired with my other sister of the heart, Jenny Moed. She liked assignments as much as I did, so we worked well together. I couldn't wait to get going with assignments. I started them as soon as they were given out. I really enjoyed researching and writing. That was a dangerous thing to say – other students probably thought I was mad, but not Jenny. She was the same, so we worked well together.

The words of Humphrey Bogart in *Casablanca* – "I think this is the beginning of a beautiful friendship" – came to mind, and that's how it turned out.

Sociology was the most interesting of subjects. My strongest memory was of an assignment in which we had to study human behaviour and present our findings to the group. One of the boys in my class performed a most memorable experiment to discover "What price dignity?" He put a five-cent coin in the bottom of the college urinal and went back the next day to see if it was still there. It was. Then he replaced the coin with a 10-cent piece. The next day it was still there. He replaced that coin with 20 cents, and the next day it had gone. My classmate concluded, "The price of dignity is about 20 cents." I still laugh when I think of that brilliant experiment.

My assignments were almost always about my experiences as a teacher's aide. I must have been a nightmare for some lecturers. I questioned the things they said when those things didn't sit well with my teaching experiences. "That's not my experience," I said – often.

Some of the lecturers had not taught children for many years. I challenged them in a polite, questioning way.

One maths teacher walked up and down the aisle with a ruler and hit it on the desk over and over. I tentatively raised my hand.

"Excuse me. I need to say something. You are not just teaching us maths. You are teaching us how to teach maths, and hitting the desk with a ruler to make students jump is not good teaching practice. Frightened children don't learn well. They need a friendly environment to thrive."

I took a deep breath and went on: "Some of us had teachers who hit us and terrorised us. I know I did. When you hit the desk and laugh at us because we jump, it's no laughing matter."

He looked at me over his glasses. I held my breath. "Quite right, too," he said, and he put the ruler away. I heaved a sigh of relief. He never hit the desk again.

In other classes, I challenged anything that didn't align with my classroom experiences. We were encouraged to debate and give opinions, and I quickly took the poster on Joan's door as my mantra: "Everyone is entitled to my opinion." I'm sure they got sick of me questioning and giving examples of my real-life situations.

Mass in the college chapel was like nothing I had experienced before. It was usually an intimate gathering in the chapel, and we gave each other Communion. Talking to the priest was lovely. He had a gentle way of making scripture relevant to our lives in the here and now. The hymns were modern and had everyone joining in with a feeling of collegiality. Occasionally, there may have been some dancing involved. College Mass was a joyous celebration, like nothing I had experienced before.

I gained a lot of insight into my spiritual self and emotional development from the religious education classes. It wasn't something I had ever thought much about before. I started to question why I acted and reacted the way I did. I questioned my core beliefs and how these dictated my responses to people and situations.

I would breeze through the door at home and announce to my children, in great detail, my new insights about religion and faith. They would look at each other and roll their eyes. Jeanette suffered in silence but not Deb.

"Oh, Mum. We get enough of that stuff at school. We don't need to hear it from you, too," she said. After that, I tried to bite my tongue and keep my insights to myself.

College was responsible for much of my faith development. It enabled me to move on from childish understandings and to read and think about life, love, forgiveness and the collegiality of the faith experience, as well as the personal nature of faith. I also studied Aboriginal spirituality – as much as any uninitiated white fella can. I found some of those beliefs and customs fascinating, and my personal understandings of the afterlife and a deity began to morph into something deeply personal.

Nobody has to agree with my philosophy. We are individuals with differing life experiences. I don't need or want anyone's approval. My philosophy grows and develops with personal experiences, reflection and meditative prayer. It is an expression of who I am. We are all on different journeys and find our way to our own individual destinations.

I don't think I have all the answers for others. I think there are "so many roads up the mountain [but] the view from the top is still the same" (to quote the Little River Band's *So Many Paths* and also possibly a Chinese proverb).

I graduated with a diploma of teaching – the first member of my family to go to college. My parents and children were so proud at my graduation that they yelled and cheered as I accepted my diploma.

"I see you've brought your cheer squad," laughed the archbishop, as he handed it to me. I was thrilled they were proud of me. Even though Mum and Dad are now gone, I still try to make up for the pain I caused them when I was 15. I try to make them as proud of me every day as they were on graduation day.

My diploma of teaching was not my last sojourn into academic life. I was later to gain a bachelor of teaching and a master's degree in history and education. The master's degree was by major focus, meaning my degree added to the body of academic work in my chosen field, rather than involving coursework. I really did like the assignments and my master's was a big one.

CHAPTER 20
My Brilliant Career

Upon graduating from Teachers' College, I hit the schools with my resume in hand and the world at my feet. As a mature age student, I had spent my college life working hard to prove I could hack the pace with the bright young things, who seemed to be able to cram enough information to pass exams in between drinks at the Laurel Hotel. Meanwhile, I slogged hard at uni and tried to be the best mother I could be at home.

Sitting in a tiny corridor outside the principal's office waiting for my first interview for a teaching job at Queen of Peace Primary School in Altona Meadows, I could see my hands shaking as I gripped my rather slim resume. Suddenly, the door opened and in walked my friend, Jenny. She was applying, too.

"I've got no hope," I thought, "I would employ Jenny if I was choosing."

We greeted each other and wished each other luck.

"I think there is more than one vacancy," Jenny smiled, "Maybe we will be teaching together?" Jenny was very chilled. She didn't seem at all nervous. I was the opposite. My stomach was in knots.

"How did you go?" I asked afterwards, expectation dripping from every word. Jenny was hesitant. She had the job of grade 4/5 teacher and was wondering whether I had missed out. Then I blurted out, "I got preps." We walked to the car park. When we were out of sight, we hugged each other excitedly with smiles reminiscent of the mouth at Luna Park.

My first day of teaching proved to be a disaster. I had been thrilled to get the prep grade and was eagerly looking forward to bonding with my new little charges and their parents. I had been so excited that I didn't sleep much the night before. On that first morning, I set up the classroom with activity stations and waited patiently for my pupils to arrive. I was blissfully unaware of the disaster that awaited me.

Me in my school teacher photo. Teaching was exhausting but it gave me plenty of laughs and fulfilment.

When families began to arrive, I welcomed them inside and asked the parents to settle their children and kiss them goodbye. The classroom was abuzz with children happily engaged in a variety of activities. Parents shed a tear as they prepared to leave their little ones – grown so quickly from babies into school children. Then came calamity. The principal stormed in and ordered the parents outside. He was angry and proceeded to roar at me for allowing the parents inside the classroom.

"If you let them in, they will want to go into every classroom and that's not your decision to make," he berated me. I cowered visibly as he aggressively pointed his finger at me. My class and the entire parent community were watching from behind the glass windows.

I was humiliated and I hadn't even started my first day of teaching.

After he stormed out, I composed myself and apologised to the parents, saying I should not have broken with school procedure. I explained I was new to the school and had no idea of the protocol. Red-faced, I turned my attention to the grade of freckle-faced darlings waiting for my undivided attention.

For a while, all ran smoothly, except for one little girl who sat in the corner sobbing, even after I coaxed her with promises of free play and drawing. Even the lure of a much-coveted gold star sticker would not tempt her to come and play with the rest of the grade. All attempts to get her to even speak to me were unsuccessful.

The poor mite looked at me with fear in her eyes and green, slimy snot running down to her chin. I made a quick dive for the tissue box and held a wad of tissues to her face. She seemed unable to blow her nose. I cleaned her face as best as I could and decided to leave her sitting on the floor. If that was what she wanted, she could stay there for now. I hoped she would see the fun the others were having and settle herself.

Meanwhile, a little boy, who had no English, began to cry. I asked him what was the matter. Using sign language, he responded by pointing in his mouth. I looked inside and saw that his throat was red and appeared swollen and, because of his obvious distress, I sent a note to the office.

"This child has a very red throat and is very distressed. Would you please contact his mother so she can check on him?" I wrote.

Back stormed the principal, nostrils flared. How dare I presume to make those kinds of decisions? The principal was the only one to decide if a parent should be called. Kindly keep your opinions to yourself was his message.

By this stage, I was nearly in tears. I apologised again and asked him to consider my request as the child was unwell and unable to communicate because of his lack of English and my lack of Italian. The principal just refused flatly, turned on his heel and swept out of the room with a wave of the hand and a "You deal with it."

I took a deep breath and composed myself, yet again, before noticing a putrid smell. I turned back to the class in time to see that the girl who had been crying in the corner had defecated in her hand and was finger painting with it all over the carpeted walls.

There was a very unpleasant cleaning job for me over lunchtime. I tried in vain to swallow the lump in my throat as I worked to remove the stains, wondering why I had spent four years in university for this.

I spent the rest of that day praying for the final bell. When it finally sounded, I talked to the mother of the little Italian boy who had been crying. He had settled now and I asked the mum to find out what had happened. It seems he had taken a drawing pin out of the wall display and swallowed it. I was stunned. Teachers' college had not prepared me for this. I asked that mother to tell the principal.

Next, I found the mother of the crying girl and said how sorry I was that her child had been upset and refused to talk to me. I told her of my efforts to make the day a good one for her but to no avail. The mother looked at me with a deep well of sadness in her eyes.

"My sweet girl can't speak. She has never, ever spoken a word to anyone. My daughter had trouble when she was born," she said.

It was obvious that she had a hard time saying those words out loud. There were medical/neurological problems that were still being investigated. Doctors were not sure how much this would affect her learning. They had informed the school of her problems. No one had bothered to tell me.

With the parents gone, I sat at my desk, overwhelmed by the events of the day. I wondered what the next day could possibly throw at me.

Since that rocky start, teaching has been a series of highs and lows. Each new grade brought with it a variety of individual personalities and challenges.

My first day was a disaster but not my worst day of teaching. That occurred at my next school, Our Lady of the Immaculate Conception, Sunshine.

It was early in the year and the preps were still learning what school was all about and how to move in large groups around the place. Some bright spark in the school administration thought it would be a good idea to book us in for swimming lessons in February when the weather was hot, obviously forgetting how unschooled preps are in their first month at school. They didn't even know how to line up. When the bell rang to signal that playtime was over, the preps ran about like ants until I gathered them up in a group to practise lining up. How was I ever going to get them to walk safely to the swimming pool in Sunshine? Thankfully, more experienced minds than mine hit upon the solution by teaming a prep with a grade 6 child for the walk. The youngsters would be in the small pool and the older children in the deeper pool.

The first day of swimming was fine and went off without a hiccup. The second day … didn't.

The tiny preppies walked, hand in hand, with their grade 6 buddies along the street. I led the way and then stood in the middle of the road to help the group cross. I told the leaders of the line of students to wait at the first tree on the other side of the road while I made sure everyone got across safely.

The leading prep child thought it would be funny to let go of her grade 6 buddy's hand and run. Off she went. Off went her grade 6 buddy after her. Off down the street ran the remaining stream of prep and grade 6 kids, with me shouting at them to stop. I caught up with the little munchkin who had started the flood and growled in my best teacher voice, which may have been accompanied by some finger-wagging. Suitably chastised, she took her place – not as leader now but further back in the line. We arrived at the pool and, as I signed the kids in at the door, one prep child ran straight through, past the change rooms and jumped into the pool – fully clothed. I fished him out and used my best teacher voice again, along with finger-wagging. I phoned his mum to bring a change of clothes and made him sit out of the lesson. He sat on the side of the pool, soaked from head to foot, crying until his mum came with dry clothes.

Meanwhile, my swimming group was restless. They were ready to get in the pool. I whipped off my outer garments to reveal my swimsuit and got in the pool. Then I realised one child was missing. He was strolling by the pool, still wearing his Y-fronts, walking funny and smelling very bad. Then he tried to get into the pool. No! I phoned his mother but got his aunt as the emergency number. She said she would bring a change of pants and other clothes (he was in a real mess), but she was fighting with his mother – her sister – so the boy might not want to talk to her. I now had a sin bin of the soaked diver and a teary defecator.

Finally, I turned my attention to my swimming group and completed their lesson, relatively uneventfully. That's if you don't count the child who was too scared to get in the water and, when I lifted her from the side of the pool, grabbed my bathers, exposing my left breast.

The walk back to school was relatively normal, but as we crossed the schoolyard, one of the ladies from the tuckshop approached me to ask about one of my students.

"Do you have Vicki?" she asked.

"Yeees," I replied very cautiously.

"Well, she has a lunch order and has written 'lollies' on the bag, $50 worth of lollies." After quickly checking that my $50 note was still in my purse, my next task was to settle the kids for lunch and phone Vicki's mum. Vicki had taken the money from the kitchen table and decided on her own lunch order for the day.

Next, I met the mother of the diver and the aunt of the Y-front boy to sort out their clothing and explain what had happened. After lunch, I was facing a group of tired five-year-olds. Now I was so frazzled that I asked the preps to sit on the carpet while I read them a story. After that, they would draw a picture and write a sentence. These tasks should not be too difficult – or at all taxing on me.

Then a shrill voice squeaked, "Simon's pissed his pants." The whole grade breathed a loud, "Ewww!" Simon sat in a puddle with a wide circle of his peers turning up their noses at him. The social pariah burst into tears. I took him aside and explained that everyone had wet their pants at some time. Even I wet my pants when I was a little girl. Wiping his tears, I gave him some dry undies to change into before he came to sit on the carpet in a dry spot.

Back to the book. I raised it to shoulder height so the kids would see the pictures and began to read. I had read one sentence when the door to the adjoining classroom flew open and in ran the teacher from next door, dragging a child behind her. The child was projectile vomiting on my carpet. At that stage, I gave up trying to teach anything at all for that day. The children could have free play while I cleaned up the urine and vomit, pondering again, why on earth I wanted to be a teacher.

Excursions

Excursions can be wonderful learning experiences for children, parents and teachers. They can also be nightmares. Most teachers spend the day on tenterhooks, trying to look nonchalant as they secretly or overtly count heads all day, in desperate fear of losing one. I never lost a child. I did, however, manage to lose a parent – twice.

For most parents, grade prep is a whole new school experience. They are not quite sure if they trust the teachers to take their children out without tagging along. A place on the excursion bus is a coveted spot. With too many wanting to come along to see the city's Christmas preparations and traditions, I had to resort to drawing out names, lucky-dip style. Unfortunately, the first name belonged to a mother who was not very reliable. When the principal asked who was accompanying us, he expressed his concern that taking this particular mum would be like taking another child along. Yet he did not want to stop her from going based on these doubts and told me to keep a close eye on her.

The big day arrived. We got to Melbourne Central in time to see Santa arrive in his sleigh and the children were delighted. We all sat down and had a snack before heading off to see the Myer window display. Every year, it was traditional for the big department store to deck out their windows in a favourite fairy tale or nursery rhyme. As we packed up our rubbish and got in line, we noticed that the mother I had been concerned about had gone. No one knew where she was or what had happened to her. Some of the other mums went off in search of her, unsuccessfully.

Time ticked on and there was still no sign of her. We had to make our next scheduled stop. By now, her son was very upset because we were moving on without his mum. Just as we were packed, lined up in twos and about to leave (half an hour behind schedule), we saw her. There she was, carrying her weekly groceries, totally oblivious to the worry she had caused. She walked up as if nothing was wrong and smiling vacantly. She had decided to go shopping and didn't think to tell anyone she was leaving the children.

I asked her not to leave the group again, explaining that coming on the excursion meant she had a responsibility to look after the children, not to go shopping. She smiled and nodded vacantly.

The next stop was Myer. The children enjoyed the window displays and then went to have an audience with Santa. While the others waited, they played in Lego World. The children were starting to get restless when the last group emerged from Santa's cottage with their colouring books and pencils. OK. All done. Let's go. I heaved a sigh of relief as I asked the kids to pack up and line up to go back to school.

Outside into the street, I did the obligatory head count. All was well. Then I saw the son of the previously errant mother holding a huge box of Lego.

"Look what my mum gave me!" he said excitedly. There was no store bag or wrapping. No receipt was taped to the box. I didn't like what was going through my mind, but I couldn't get away from that shop quickly enough. I was just so relieved that no store detective stopped us.

The next time I lost a parent was at the Melbourne Zoo. We had a lovely day. The clouds that had threatened to ruin our excursion had dissolved into beautiful sunshine. Getting there went well, and the children were safe with their group leaders. They were very well-behaved and enjoyed a great learning experience. We met back at the lunch pavilions and couldn't believe our eyes. The laundry baskets of lunches we had left there had been attacked by seagulls, and lunches were strewn all over the ground. We salvaged what we could and shared what was left among all of the kids.

After lunch, it was time to head home. Once on the bus, I counted heads. All 29 children were present and correct. I told the driver to take us home and slumped into a seat at the front of the bus. About 10 minutes into the journey, the driver got a call on his radio. We had left one of the mothers back at the zoo. She had gone to return something to the front office and missed the bus. I couldn't believe I had left her there. I messaged her to grab a taxi and charge the school.

Unfortunately, the principal didn't agree. I had to pay for my mistake by paying for the cab fare.

CHAPTER 21
Out of the Mouths of Babes

I have spent most of my working life teaching in Catholic schools, where I have been responsible for the children's religious education and sometimes that of parents and teachers as well. Existential beings and a sense of self as a spiritual entity are too complex for most adults to understand, let alone kids. Religion is often a source of confusion and a mystery to the little ones, but they bring their ideas to the discussion. Some have never been inside a church or even heard the word "God" when they begin their Catholic school lives. This became clear during prayer times when children's misheard utterances were the source of much teacher merriment – with a bitten lip of course.

Many of the prep children have never been inside a church. I was preparing my little charges to be quiet during their first visit to church.

"We are going into God's house. When you go inside God's house you talk to God quietly in your hearts."

As we turned to watch the priest walk down the aisle for Mass, one child yelled excitedly at the top of her voice, "I know that God!"

Another child asked a very profound question: "Why wasn't Jesus a girl?" I had to

The Wicked Queen from Snow White during Book Week.

dig into my knowledge of history for an answer. My answer: "That's a great question. I think it was because back then, men didn't listen to women and girls. They only listened to other men."

When kids say the most delightful and funniest of things, the teacher should never laugh at them but rather smile and bite her lip to avoid embarrassing them – better a teacher's bruised lip than a child's bruised ego.

Some of these memorable moments made the load I carried as a teacher not only worthwhile but joyous. Whenever I was so busy that I was counting the number of yard duties until the holidays, or so stressed that I considered chucking it all in, some wonderful child brightened my day with a gem. These words lifted my spirits and made me soar through another hectic day.

Here are some of the children's slip-ups and observations, as experienced in my classroom.

The grade 1 students were very rowdy:
Me: "Now settle down and work. You're too restless."
A small boy: "Who are they?"
Me: "What do you mean?"
Boy: "Who are the two wrestlers?"

Then the day before a public holiday:
Me: "There's no school tomorrow."

One boy jumped up, yelling:
"Yay! We're going to the snow. There's snow school tomorrow."

A child was showing me his book of anatomy and indicating the internal organs. He was around six years old:
"This is his heart, this is his stomach, and this is his intesticles [intestines]."
I had to bite my lip to avoid laughter at that moment.

A five-year-old brought a book to school for show and tell:
"My book is called Beauty and the Bitch."

Not one other child reacted.
I quietly whispered in her ear:
"Beast. Beauty and the Beast."
She didn't believe me.

A confused prep child looked at my lunch order:
"*Ms Lane, why do you always have a salad roll for your lunch? Can't you spell pie?*"

In the playground, I overheard a prep child's mother say to her son:
"*Do you have free play at your school?*"
His younger brother interrupted:
"*We have four-play at my kinder.*"

Show and tell can get parents into all sorts of trouble. One of my colleagues, Jennifer, came to the door that separated our two classrooms with tears of laughter in her eyes:
"*Oh, Maureen. I have to tell someone. Johnny just had show and tell.*"
By now, the tears had made their way to her chin.
"*He said, 'My mum and dad had to have a shower together because we don't have much soap.'*"
Then we both had tears of laughter.

My pal, Jenny, told me her show and tell story:

A little girl rose with a sad expression on her face:
"*My dad has been gone for three nights and we don't know where he is.*"
Another child called out: "*He's at our house.*"

Of course, the kids aren't the only ones who say the wrong thing or get the wrong idea. I've been guilty of that a few times.
Once I was aware the garlic pasta I had the previous evening had probably given me garlic breath. I doused myself with perfume and brushed my teeth vigorously. While sitting up close to one of the children, listening to him read, the words I had dreaded came from his mouth:
"You smell funny."
I felt the red heat of shame rise on my face and went into a long explanation.
"I had garlic in my dinner last night, and that has made my breath smell a bit stinky," I apologised profusely.
Innocently, he replied: "I thought it was perfume."
Spoonerisms – which occur when the first letters of words are swapped, usually by accident, to make different words – can get people into a lot of trouble. Things like "chish and fips" for fish and chips or "palt and sepper" for salt and pepper.
I will never forget a spoonerism that popped out in front of my fourth-grade students. We had a lesson on the Old Testament and King David. Most of the kids had been to the movies to see the cartoon version of King David, so they were familiar with his regal role in the Bible. I wanted them to know he had been a poor boy:
"David wasn't always a king. He was a shepherd boy," I said, but I was confronted

by blank looks – they didn't know what a shepherd was. I tried to enlighten them with hilarious results.

"A shepherd boy – he would shit in the fields with the seep." There was stunned silence from most and an audible gasp from others.

"Oh, my goodness. I'm so sorry. I didn't mean that. I meant to sit in the fields with the sheep." An explanation of spoonerisms followed, but it was too late. The damage was done. I was a laughing stock.

I managed to embarrass myself quite a lot in front of the kids and parents, but the worst example occurred while I was doing a Bible reading from the lectern in church, in front of the whole school community. The text read, "Love is never selfish," but I read, "Love is never shellfish." With scarlet cheeks, I took a deep breath and carried on to the end of the reading, hoping no one would notice. They did. My colleagues never let me forget it.

Despite these slips, I decided to enrol in university and obtain a master's degree in education. I was fairly confident I could perform well enough to gain the additional qualification. I hoped it might lead to a future job as a principal.

I chose the history of education, combining my love of Australian history with research on education.

At the time, I was teaching at a Catholic school in Sunshine that had lost its history when the old church, which doubled as a schoolroom, went up in smoke. It was quite a challenge, but I managed to track down some octogenarians who had started their education at the local state school and transferred. One former pupil explained the recruitment procedure.

"The priest came into our classroom and pointed to me and then other kids in the room and said 'You. You. You. All come with me." He marched us out of the school and down the street to the church that was just a one-room building. After that, it was our school."

I discovered the state school, miraculously, had preserved its old attendance rolls in an archive. In these, I found the date on which the octogenarians had left the school; then I identified all the other students who had departed on the same day, thereby compiling a student list used for the opening of the Catholic school.

After that, I pieced together a fairly comprehensive history of that school and extrapolated information about other schools in the area. I loved writing the thesis and felt ready to tackle the world. I loved my job, I wanted to advance my career and that principalship seemed a little closer.

CHAPTER 22
Relationships

"Why do you want an annulment from the church?" asked the cannon lawyer, peering over the tops of glasses that sat halfway down his nose.

It was a big question. I didn't want to give the answer to a stranger, a celibate male who looked at me as if I was dirt. Nevertheless, I fronted up to his office and answered his questions. While answering his embarrassing questions, I became aware there was a large painting of a ship in a storm behind the lawyer's head.

"Is that a picture of a sinking ship?" I asked. "Does it mean that we, who sit in this chair answering questions, are drowning, going down with the ship?"

The lawyer looked a little annoyed and then amused.

"Oh, no. It is supposed to mean 'weathering a storm'… I think," he said.

I visited that office many times and jumped through the required hoops. I gathered witnesses and wrote accounts of my marriage to Fred. One day, when I had a late appointment, I went to the movies in town before seeing the lawyer. The movie, *The Killing Fields*, dealt with the slaughter of innocents in Cambodia.

Sitting in a darkened theatre tears cascaded down my cheeks. It was a harrowing experience. Outside afterwards, when the sunlight hit my red eyes, I squinted and put on sunglasses, as much to hide my eyes as for sun protection. With each step towards the office, I reflected on the hugeness of the Cambodia experience compared to my little life-marriage story.

I sat in the chair and, after pleasantries, said:

"I've just been to see *The Killing Fields*. I really don't care if you grant me an annulment or not. The world is full of terrible things and my problems don't seem that big right now. I know in my very being that a loving Father would not condemn a 15-year-old to a brutal and loveless marriage – even after she had left the situation. I know that my relationship with God is bigger and more important than a piece of paper that you hold in your hand. Give me an annulment or not. I will be content that I have done the right thing leaving that marriage and I know *my* loving Father wants me to be happy."

"Don't give up. Please," he said, looking concerned.

I replied: "I won't give up on my faith, but this process is not important to me anymore."

Thanking him for his time and effort, I left for the train home. Three weeks later, a notice came in the mail. I had an annulment from the Catholic Church.

I was celibate for eight years until I met Tony. We met at a church dance and moved in together when my girls were grown up and had moved out. I loved Tony, and I think he loved me, in his way. He won me over at our first meeting.

"I've got a couple of free tickets to see a movie. Would you like to come with me?" I could never say no to a movie.

Tony was good company, and I looked after him in much the same way I had cared for my children. He was very money-conscious, though, and if there were things that needed fixing around the house, I usually paid for them. We purchased a three-bedroom home in Pascoe Vale, and I replaced the carpet, the wallpaper and the stove and painted the walls in the kitchen.

Long time friends. From left: Rod, Joan, Angela, Kriss, Melissa, Jeff, Clara and Saverio.
Photo: Mark Phillips.

I was happy to cook the meals and do the shopping, but Tony insisted we split the bills, so he would expect me to put receipts on the fridge under a magnet where he would place his half in cash – to the cent. I didn't worry about money. I had been very poor while at teachers' college and felt very privileged to have a full pay packet every week. I had been looking after my kids for 20 years, so I guess my nurturing nature took over with Tony.

We were good company for each other, and he had a great group of friends who loved to socialise. Paula, Jim, Nicky, Maria, Karl, Graeme, Kelly Anne, Melissa, Steve, Angela, Don and Rowdy Rod were the mainstays, and others joined or left the group at different times.

Jeff and Joan were leaders of the "Rat Pack," as Jeff liked to call us. We had card nights at their home quite often, played Uno and ate fish and chips. I held parties at our house. We had Halloween and dinner parties at which everyone brought a plate of goodies to share. It was great fun and we all got along very well.

Tony and I were going away for a weekend and I had the idea of asking the Rat Pack along. I put the call out and said we could let them know where we were staying and they could book rooms, too.

They were all interested and so a dozen or so of us started going away, exploring

Victoria's beautiful countryside together, staying overnight and then coming back a day or two later. I enjoyed being the organiser, and everyone was really appreciative of my efforts.

Of all the weekends we spent together, the "ghost house" stood out from the rest.

"There's an abandoned mental hospital at Beechworth and I'd love to go there," Paula said.

Paula was the adventurer in the group and very keen to explore and hunt the ghosts that might lurk in the corners of a spooky abandoned cell block. Not all the rooms had been renovated and the rumour was that those were untouched for good reason.

Heading north on a Saturday morning, some of us were in what could loosely be called a convoy. Others made their way alone to the imposing white building in the country township of Beechworth.

"Hello? Anyone there?" We stood in the foyer and waited. Tony rang the bell on the desk, and we started to wonder where everyone was.

"This is like the start of a horror movie," someone suggested, and we giggled nervously. I shifted uneasily from foot to foot as we waited.

"Hello, can I help you?" A bright and cheery woman in her mid-thirties checked us in.

"I hope you don't mind, but you won't be in the main hotel," she said.

"We have put your party all together in one of the outbuildings. It's been renovated, but the rooms are very small. It's the old staff quarters and it has its own kitchen and courtyard. I'm sure you will be very comfortable there."

We carried our bags up the steps to the big double doors. It was then that we noticed the lock was on the outside. "Hmm ... staff quarters? I think not."

We opened the door and piled inside a huge lounge room. There was plenty of room for all of us to sit and watch TV or play cards at the huge dining table. A corridor led us around a square to the kitchen and courtyard. Tiny cell-like bedrooms jutted off the corridor and, even in daylight, the place had an eerie feel.

The first night, we couldn't get warm. We had the heater turned up full but huddled in the lounge with coats and blankets around us trying to play Uno – something that always made everyone laugh and tease each other with joking comments: "Hurry up. Pensions mounting," or "I've got a hand like a foot." When someone had to pick up cards instead of playing them, there would be a chorus of "Sacrificing." We played as long as we could but gave up battling the cold and said our goodnights, making our way to our cells to get warm under the blankets.

I was the first to hear it. "Click ... Click ... Click ..."

"Tony!" I jabbed him in the ribs. "What's that?"

"I don't know. Go back to sleep," he replied with a half-open eye.

Listening in the darkness to the clicking noise, my eyes were like saucers as I watched the door through the darkness. Eventually, I summoned enough courage to grab my trusty torch and, in bare feet on bare boards, I propelled myself nervously towards the noise. I stopped at a door and listened. "Click ... Click ... Click ..." It was coming from Paula and Jim's room.

"Roll over, Jim." It was Paula's voice piercing the darkness.

The weird noise was coming from her husband, who didn't snore but made a strange sound in his throat that was amplified through the halls, the effect heightened by earlier tales of Ghosties and Goosebumps.

"Paula. Jim had me worried out of my head. I couldn't work out what that noise was," I whispered through the door.

"It had me flummoxed at first, too, but it's just Jim making a funny noise in his sleep. Don't worry. Night night." Paula gave Jim a jab to the ribs, and he rolled over, ending his night-time one-legged ghost impressions.

The next morning at breakfast, we had a good laugh at ourselves. Those who heard the noise but didn't leave the safety of their tiny cells and those who slept right through thought I was mad to go exploring in the darkness when our accommodation only had locks on the outside of the front door.

Jim was a bit embarrassed but laughed. Then Melissa joined us for breakfast, and we asked her if she had heard the ghost last night.

"Someone sat on the end of my bed in the middle of the night pretending to be a ghost. Who was it?" We all shot sideways glances at each other and there was an uneasy silence. No one owned up.

The next day, we went exploring historic Beechworth. We visited the old jail and courthouse where the famous bushranger, Ned Kelly, was first tried and convicted, beginning a life of crime that would catapult him into Australian folklore.

We watched a night performance by the local dramatic society and delved into the history of the area and its gold mining days. It would have been a good night except for Rowdy Rod, who must have over indulged in a particularly spicy curry. Little tooting sounds were emitting from his general direction and wafting odours hung heavy in the air. I was seated next to him. It made the performance seem unending. I was glad to get out into the crisp night air and go back to my little cell.

That night, indoors was less eventful than the first, but instead of us shivering, the heater was working overtime, and we were all cooking in the lounge. The controls had not changed since the night before, but the temperature difference was huge. We got a bit spooked and had an early night, being sure to shut our cell doors.

After an uneventful night and breakfast that included a Bee Sting, a delicious sweet bun – filled with custard and topped with slithers of almonds and a drizzle of honey – from the famous Beechworth Bakery, we headed home. It had been an adventure we would never forget.

Beechworth was only one of many weekends away. We had fun together, exploring and creating wonderful memories.

I loved my life. I had a leadership role at a Diamond Creek primary school and was teaching grade 1. I didn't want to get married again. I was happy in our relationship and so was Tony. I was part of a Rat Pack, a friendship family that would remain close for the next 40 years and more.

Tony and I both loved travelling, and we drove from Melbourne up north to Cairns, flew to Darwin to visit his cousins and flew back to Cairns to drive home via the scenic ocean road route, sharing the journey with one of our pals, Damian, for some of the way.

Damian had been Tony's school friend and flatmate. He became a good friend to me as well. I could always rely on him for a laugh and he was good company and when times got tough, Damian was always on the other end of the phone to check in on me.

Tony and I travelled to Japan and America and shared a lot of exciting experiences. We made some beautiful memories. I thought Tony would be my forever partner, but it was not to be.

Damian.

CHAPTER 23
Accidental Madness

I loved teaching at the Diamond Creek primary school where I taught prep to grade 4 students. The principal, Anne, had a lot of faith in me and gave me the position of religious education leader within the leadership team. In this role, I helped decide the school's direction. I instigated changes designed to give our students and teachers meaningful experiences and help them develop skills, knowledge and an understanding of spirituality.

It was at Sacred Heart Diamond Creek that I obtained funding from the Catholic Education Office to involve the local Indigenous community and develop the Aboriginal Perspectives Across the Curriculum program.

The project took a year to complete. I gave a presentation on it at the Peace and Justice Seminar at Melbourne University, where it was well received and attracted a lot of interest. My program was developed with the help of Indigenous people from Diamond Creek and surrounding areas. It incorporated research about other groups' customs and traditions. Aboriginal Perspectives was part of each subject at school rather than what was insultingly called "Doing Aborigines," where teachers would present information and activities about our Indigenous people. Many of these tokenistic classes had only a tenuous link to Indigenous culture or had a "white-washed" undertone.

My program was designed to build respect for differences while highlighting similarities between two Australian belief systems. For example, when our children were learning about baptism, one of the rites of initiation in the Catholic Church, we would also mention spiritual ceremonies that link babies to the earth in some communities in Central Australia and elsewhere.

When the children were preparing for their Confirmation, a ceremony that acknowledges the spiritual transition into adulthood, we would bring attention to Indigenous rites of initiation practised by other communities. Some are so sacred that they cannot be known by outsiders.

I taught my grade four days a week and worked as a religious education coordinator one day a week. I had a liturgy team of volunteer students to assist in planning school Masses and other religious celebrations and practices. They met me at lunchtime before each special event to plan and make sure the Mass was as smooth, as prayerful and as much fun as possible.

I loved my job. I was at school from 8.15am to 5pm, or later, every night. Then I would go home and cook a meal for myself and Tony. I never told anyone at school about Tony. If details of that relationship were to become common knowledge, it would have been grounds for dismissal. The fact that we lived together remained a secret.

In June, 2003, my friend and colleague, Katrina, was preparing for the annual concert. Movie Music through the Decades was the theme. Our grades were focusing on the 1950s by performing a rock'n'roll dance to the Bill Haley classic *Rock Around the Clock* and a waltz to *Shall We Dance* from *The King and I*.

Our grades rehearsed in the school's big hall, where the concert would take place, to teach them the lyrics and dance moves. On one occasion, the kids were lined up excitedly at the hall door, waiting to come in.

"Settle down. You can't go indoors making all that noise," I said in my best teacher's voice.

As I stood waiting for the children to settle, I was unaware that this moment would impact the rest of my life.

Katrina and I stood in the doorway, but I was directly under the closing mechanism and arm fitted to the top of the door. Suddenly, the whole thing gave way and hit me on the head with a "thump."

"Ouch!" I reached up to rub my head. The kids all laughed.

"Quiet down. We can't go in until you are quiet," I said.

Katrina was looking at me with wide eyes, "Maureen. There's blood."

I touched my head again and realised my hand was covered in blood.

"You have to go to the office," Katrina continued.

Dazed, I made my way to the front office, getting more confused with each step. The secretary was on the phone and waved me towards the sick bay, but it was overflowing with ill or malingering children. I lay on the couch in the staff room and drifted into unconsciousness.

I woke as the priest tramped through the lounge area.

"Don't you look dramatic lying there," he said.

"The door closer in the hall hit me on the head." I directed my comment in the general direction of the doorway where he stood. I couldn't see very clearly, but I knew who it was.

"I'll go and fix that," he said, and he strode out, leaving me still unattended.

I slipped back to sleep until another teacher, Libby, came in for lunch.

"Are you alright?" she asked. Her brow furrowed and eyes uncertain.

"I don't think I am," I said.

The rest is a bit of a blur.

I know Libby took me to the doctor. I know someone drove me home. I know I was lying on my couch alone at 7.30pm when Tony came home. I didn't have the presence of mind to call my daughters before then. I guess I drifted in and out of consciousness. When I was awake, as the old saying goes, "The lights were on, but nobody was home."

The official diagnosis was "concussion," but my family soon realised it was a lot more. I would spend hours looking at the TV but not seeing it. I couldn't concentrate on anything.

I tried to go back to work after two weeks, but on the way there, I nearly drove my car off the road and returned home. I got lost. I was living in a fog and felt sick. Something was very wrong.

Deb said, "Mum, I knew there was something really wrong when you stopped calling us to talk about current affairs and you stopped telling jokes."

Deb moved in with us for a little while to look after me, although I can't remember that. My mind was a muddle. Having put so much store in my education and mental abilities, I now had lost the ability to remember large pieces of my past and I couldn't even recall my own phone number. I couldn't talk on the phone or write a message – or anything else that required doing two tasks at once. Maths was a big frustration – I couldn't add or subtract. Worst of all, every time I moved around, I became so sick and dizzy that I had to stop and sit still. I spent a lot of time staring at the TV in the corner of the room without really knowing what was happening in the story.

"Maureen, you have an ABI. An acquired brain injury." I heard the words coming out of my doctor's mouth, but I couldn't comprehend the meaning. "It may get a little better in time, but you are unlikely to be able to continue teaching."

The words swam in my head. I thought I must have misheard what was just said. I often lost the plot when people talked to me, so I thought I must have done that again, but no.

"Your brain has a permanent injury," the doctor said. "You can do some more rehab and we can manage the headaches with pain relief, but you will always have the difficulties you have now. They may improve but it is not likely they will ever resolve."

Tony started staying later at work or having dinner with his work friends. I spent a lot of time alone as I did rehabilitation sessions to try to get my brain back online. Eventually, with the help of an occupational therapist, I was able to go shopping, but trying to locate an item on the shelf was a whole new nightmare. To find a label, I had to read every single label to locate what I was looking for. I could not simply pick out a packet or tin from an array without the laborious task of examining every one until I came across the right one. After a visit to the supermarket, I was exhausted.

Shopping also caused me some embarrassment. I must have really liked the little shorts and T-shirt in the window of the local babywear shop because I purchased them for my little grandson, Conor – twice.

"Mum," said Deb, "You already gave him this."

"No, I just bought it," I replied. Then she produced the exact same outfit. I was embarrassed and alarmed. I wasn't doing as well as I had thought.

Eventually, I returned to work "on light duties," and they welcomed me with open arms. I wasn't able to teach a grade – if I couldn't pick out a tin of baked beans from the shelf, how could I pick out a child from the group? The principal was lovely to me and so was every person in the school, inquiring about my health.

"All better now?"

Of course, I wasn't, but I couldn't go into details, so I would just say, "Yes, thank you."

My light duties involved my religious education coordinator's role – mostly writing. I hadn't lost that ability, and I could spend as much time as it required on editing.

My head injury stopped me from having the fun times I had enjoyed with friends and family. I couldn't walk far without feeling dizzy. Crowds were overwhelming, so Deb and I stopped going to see my beloved North Melbourne Kangaroos play football – a tradition that had been started by my father and his father way back before our club was called North Melbourne (1882) when they were known as Hotham Football Club.

That was a very sad loss of a family tradition for me.

Shopping crowds were a nightmare. I felt as if people were heading straight for me and I was afraid of being bumped off balance and ending up on the floor.

My friends stopped asking me to go out for dinner. Restaurants were crowded. Unable to scan the room, I would stand in the doorway until someone noticed I was there and made contact with me.

My sight in any crowd was a jumble of blurred faces and I could not isolate individuals in my line of vision. Eventually, I worked out that if I waited to be noticed at the door and then sat at a table with my back to the crowd, I could concentrate on the person in front of me and block out the rest of the room. That was until it got too noisy and I was forced to make an excuse and leave.

Often, I sat outside in a cab with tears cascading down my cheeks, trying to compose myself – sad and angry that I had lost the person I used to be. I had become someone else. I was no longer the academic student, teacher, historian or caregiver that I had always been. Now I couldn't teach a grade or even talk on the phone. Writing messages to myself was difficult, and these were very important because my memory was in constant fog. Now I was a patient and a burden.

I developed sleep apnoea and woke multiple times during the night gasping for breath. Of course, I woke hundreds more times without realising my sleep was disturbed. My breathing stopped many times in every REM sleep minute. I woke with a migraine and that contributed to my confusion. When my doctor finally realised what was wrong, I got a CPAP machine to help me breathe through the night.

Instead of being the caregiver in our family, I became a patient, but mostly looked after myself as best I could.

Tony decided to leave his job to take another opportunity in the same field of finance. He was going to his farewell party and preparing himself for a big night out, so he wanted me to drive him. With a chauffeur, he could have more than a few drinks and enjoy saying goodbye to that friendship group.

I got behind the wheel and started the car, but as I drove down the road, it kept swerving slightly to the left, over and over, until I ran the car up onto the kerb.

"I can't do this, Tony. I can't drive. I'm not well enough," I said.

"That's alright," Tony replied. "The station is just there. I'll catch the train." I struggled to keep the car on the road as I made my way home at a snail's pace.

At the time, I didn't realise how careless and callous Tony's response had been. I went home and cried. I knew I was not getting any better.

It wasn't until a visit from my friend, Angela, that I realised how self-absorbed Tony's response was that day.

"I tried to go to the party but kept driving onto the footpath," I told Angela. "So Tony caught the train and I managed to get myself home. I have always prided myself on being a good driver, but it's a miracle I didn't have an accident. I have been driving since I was 21, but now I can't even stay on the road."

Angela's simple question turned my life upside down.

"Why didn't Tony drive you?"

The light bulb went off with a flash and suddenly I knew that Tony did not love me. I was the giver in this relationship, and he was a taker. When the roles reversed, he didn't have anything to give.

I'd lived with Tony for 16 years, taking care of him, and he was never, ever going to take care of me because he didn't love me.

I cried a lot. I talked to Tony.

"You have changed too much," Tony said. "I just want to stay here in the house. You are the kindest person I know, but we should just do our own thing."

"What happened to me wasn't my fault," I pleaded. "If I could be the same as I was, I would, but I can't." There were more tears, and the sadder I got, the more confused my mind became and the more distant Tony became.

My psychologist suggested that Tony come to a session so he could understand what was happening to me.

Tony was late walking into the office. He sat as far away from me as he could. He was feeling as if he was being blamed for his reaction to my illness and that the psychologist and I were ganging up on him.

Finally, the psychologist said to Tony: "What do you want Maureen to do?"

"Nothing," he replied.

She asked me what I wanted Tony to do.

"Take me on a date," I replied. "Plan it and take me somewhere for dinner."

He agreed and we left the office.

He never took me on that date.

It was over.

Angela opened my eyes and has remained a confidante.
Photo: Mark Phillips.

CHAPTER 24
Buffy to the Rescue

Tony and I continued to share the house, but we were not a couple anymore. Of course, Tony was right. I was not the person I used to be. She died under the weight of the door closer when it hit me. I grieved for the person I had been. I had to come to terms with the fact that I was gone.

My old self, moulded by my past experiences and achievements, was no longer me. A dark cloud of depression settled over me, but I tried to fake it and hide that from everyone. My self-esteem was at an all-time low. I had lost faith in the abilities I still had. I began to doubt everything that I remembered. Self-doubt plagued me. Every day I pretended I was OK and every day my mind was in turmoil.

Desperately, I tried to find things to occupy my mind, but the dizzy spells limited me physically. It was hard to know how I could get my mind back on track. Help came in an unusual package.

The one thing that kept me company and relatively sane was TV. Being able to concentrate on TV was a small sign I had made progress.

Feeling lost and lonely, I turned on the television to get involved in someone else's story. I could become a different person for an hour or two, experience things and go places while not moving from the safety of my couch.

"*Buffy the Vampire Slayer* – what a silly name," I thought. "That might be worth a laugh, and I could really do with a laugh – even a smile would do."

From that first viewing, when the helpless teenage girl was stalked by vampires but transformed into a powerhouse of self-defence, I knew that this show broke the mould. I was hooked.

Although *Buffy* was aimed at teens, I found I could concentrate on it even though I had a great deal of difficulty with other focusing tasks.

The heroine was a young girl who could do remarkable and often altruistic things to save the world. It was funny, exciting and character-driven. I got to know and love that show and all its characters. I also recognised the allegory within the episodes.

That love of *Buffy* took me to the internet, where I typed in *Buffy the Vampire Slayer* and up came an Australian online forum where people talked about each episode and chatted about all things nerdy relating to *Buffy* and, occasionally, deeper aspects of filmmaking and story writing.

Mostly they just seemed to have fun and enjoy each other's company, and I desperately needed company. I had never joined a forum before.

At first, I just read the comments until I got enough courage to post an opinion. I must have rewritten my first post a dozen times before posting to be sure my brain wasn't doing loops and I was actually making sense.

The *Buffy* forum let me talk to people from the safety of my own home. They were a warm and friendly group who shared my obsession. The group welcomed me as one of their own. When a *Buffy* convention was held in Melbourne, some of the actors came to talk and sign autographs. My daughter's friend, Sheri, who shared my *Buffy* obsession, said she would take me.

Fun times at the conventions with the Buffy crew.

My Buffy parties with new found friends who helped me get through a very tough time.

At the convention centre, I came face to face with actors from the show and bumped into people I knew from the forum. Their enthusiasm was infectious and I became even more swept up in the excitement. I began attending every *Buffy* forum and some *Star Trek* forums too, having amazing experiences and creating precious memories.

What began as a tentative, unfamiliar computer experience related to a TV show became a source of constant online companionship. Eventually, those in the forums became my regular in-person friends.

When the spin-off series *Angel* came to Foxtel, I invited the group to come to watch it at my house. Every Thursday night, five to 15 *Buffy/Angel* fans assembled in my lounge room, ate pizza and watched *Angel* before dissecting each scene and the storyline. My young friends were fun, and this was another step towards some kind of recovery from my acquired brain injury.

When Tony came home from work, he tried to join the party, but I asked him to respect my privacy. I felt a bit mean, but he had his own life without me and I was desperately trying to create a life without him.

At 9.30pm, it was "chucking out time" because I was back at work three days a week and needed to have my wits about me to concentrate the next day. As the clock ticked over, I showed them the door with the promise of "See you next week."

Those young people became very important to me. Blue Meanie, Gemini Webster, Harm, Elyn, klvn, grsxboy, Shar, Dirty Rotten Bomber, Puppy, Ainsley, Ali Em, Alie, Andree, Neets, Boffin Pope, Charley, Faith, Heather, Bellos, Lisa, Ian, Marina, Marion, Mel, Nathan, Suze, Shad, Antoinette, Kirsten, Terry, Lisa and many others. They understood my limitations and didn't seem to mind. These young people embraced me and included me in their parties, even though I was old enough to be their mother.

Spike2 was one of the members of this group who would always offer to give me a lift in his car, and he made sure I was able to get home. When I had a sensory overload and needed to leave, there would be that friendly face to drive me home.

These youngsters accepted me as one of their own and I felt comfortable in their company. Spike2, grsxboy, Blue Meanie, Elyn and especially Harm, have remained my close friends over the years.

Friendships made in that group have endured more than 20 years. Some highlights for me have been: going to Western Australia with Blue Meanie and having grsxboy rescue us and let us stay with him when our hotel had bedbugs; hanging out with Harm (Dana) and sharing secrets; and travelling with Son of Acathla, an American boy from Kentucky whose mother asked me to take him under my wing. We saw all the tourist sites and I had great fun being a tour guide. When Son of Acathla got married, I received an invitation to the wedding, but my health did not allow me to go. I've always regretted that. I was devastated when I learnt of his sudden death a few years later.

Being invited to the wedding supper of Buffy kids, Elyn and Dean, was a big thrill and an honour. They had been married in Las Vegas by an Elvis impersonator and had their reception in a Melbourne café where a film of their Vegas extravaganza was shown on a big screen. It was such a fun night. I was able to stay for most of it, which gave me hope that my injuries might be more manageable, in time.

After the excitement of yet another *Buffy* convention with the gang, we went to the Crown Bar for a drink. We were chatting excitedly

Buffy friends would come over but needed to go by 9pm otherwise I could not function at work the next day.

about the show that Anthony Stewart Head had put on. He had sung *Sweet Transvestite* and brought the house down with his portrayal of Frank-N-Furter from *Rocky Horror Picture Show*. James Marsters had been gracious and signed autographs and chatted to everyone and we were still buzzing. Then, Son of Acathla spotted both of them at the bar.

"There they are. I'm going to buy them a drink," he said.

We followed him over to say hello and chat for a while. They were very gracious and candid, answering all our questions, and I even got a hug from both of them before they had to go. It was a night to remember for all of us, apparently – they told the organisers what a good time they had with us.

My dear friend and penpal, Kris whom I met on the *Buffy* forum. He holidayed in Australia so we could meet him and we showed him around.

The Buffy gang meets Anthony "Giles" Head and James "Spike" Marsters at a Crown bar. From left: Chris (Spike 2), Son of Acathla, me, Anthony Head, Dana (Harm), James Marsters, and Kirsten.

CHAPTER 25
Trial by Jury

Time had little meaning for me after my head injury. Seldom did I know what day it was, and the hour meant nothing at all. Sleep was elusive, so I was awake until the early hours of the morning and slept when I was too exhausted to keep my eyes open. I travelled to work in a taxi because I couldn't drive far without getting lost. Another horrible symptom of my brain injury was that I couldn't abide listening to music in the car or elsewhere. The sensory overload made me feel as if the music was jumbling my brain. Driving to the corner shop required all my concentration, so even that had to be done in silence.

The time came for a judge to hear my WorkCover case, and I was enveloped in a cloud of confusion. I was running out of money. Living on my savings and the small stipend that WorkCover provided was difficult.

"Would Ms Lane take the stand?" I was beckoned to the wooden structure to the left of the judge.

This judge had a chat with the opposing counsel, as "in the spirit of full disclosure" he had worked for the same WorkCover lawyers that now lined up against me. He was congenial and smiled warmly at the opposing counsel, no doubt reminiscing about his days arguing against WorkCover claims like mine.

Along with the WorkCover solicitors, I had to face the Catholic Church's solicitors. My counsel suggested that they were there in great numbers as this would be a test case for the expected onslaught of child molestation cases on Church property. I had been injured on Church property, so there was a parallel to be drawn.

My two barristers and two clerks went into battle for me against a team of about eight people who were watching my every move and ready to pounce.

The clerk of the courts beckoned me again, and I picked my way through the minefield of briefcases and papers and feet, trying to maintain my precarious balance as I made it to the stand.

A jumble of thoughts went through my mind: "What did he just ask me? Are those people on the jury going to listen and understand me? Will the judge be fair? How can I do this? I feel embarrassed. I spend my life hiding my incapacities and now I have to lay them bare for the whole courtroom, and the world, to scrutinise, so they can try to prove I am a liar."

My spirit was crushed by each loaded question that tried to insinuate I had somehow plotted to have this happen to me or that I was faking my condition. They wanted to know about my sex life and relationship. They wanted to know how proficient I was on the computer. I told them I had not lost my ability to write but the workings of computers remained much of a mystery to me. They continued to charge me with "crimes" of belonging to the *Buffy* website. They showed photos of me at my home dressed in a Halloween costume. I tried to explain that I hosted the party because I couldn't go out and battle nighttime driving. It fell on deaf ears and the next accusation floored me. They suggested I might be a lesbian. I was surprised at that, but the fact I had dressed as Jack Sparrow for Book Week at school and recycled the costume for the Halloween party seemed damning evidence to them. I simply said "No." I wondered why, if that were true, that would have been an issue anyway. Apparently, it might sway a Catholic jury – according to my counsel.

I have always tried to do what is right, and here I was in a public courtroom being accused of being a charlatan of the worst order, by the Church I had worked for and whose people I had loved all my life.

Pompous men stood like barnyard roosters, chests puffed out and pecking at me as I faced accusations of faking the symptoms of my illness and being a woman of "loose morals."

With every word I was stripped of my dignity, and my protests were like snow on a summer's day.

The first day in court, I was questioned for four hours, causing sensory overload. I was on the verge of tears with every breath. The next day was another three hours before I broke down and wept. I had no strength left. My vision was blurred, and my head thumped. I was broken in body and spirit.

My barrister did his best to bat away the arrows that were fired at me, wounding my soul. Eventually, I could take it no more and settled out of court for a fraction of what my claim should have been.

For losing the social life I loved, my partner of 16 years and the job I had excelled at, I received about two-and-a-half years' pay.

God love my barristers; they waived their fee when they saw the pittance that I accepted was not even enough to cover my lost wages thus far. My solicitors did not waive their fees. I had not accessed Centrelink payments, so my bank balance was already sparse. I had expected to get justice, but that was not to be.

After the settlement was begrudgingly agreed upon, I insisted on letting the jury know that my employer had accepted responsibility by the very act of settling. I wanted them to know that all those evil things said about me in court were not true. Some jury members gave me a nod and a big smile while one gentleman even gave me a thumbs up in support. It eased the huge weight of "rocks" the trial caused me to carry, but even to this day, they are a burden on my back.

For every rock, there is a feather. Throughout this trauma my darling daughters were very supportive. Jeanette cooked meals for me and looked after Deborah's boys so she could come with me to court every single day. Some days, Deborah brought her baby son, Dan. She held him and my hand to comfort me.

After the case had concluded, the barrister for the Church came and spoke to Deborah.

"If ever something as terrible as what happened to your mother happened to me, I would hope my children would show me the same love and support that you displayed during the case," he said.

He turned to join the smiling ranks of the opposition counsel as they congratulated each other for wearing me down and on the pittance that I had accepted to make it all stop.

CHAPTER 26
The Dating Game

The devastation of my breakup with Tony and the court case worsened my health. Eventually, the impact of these events began to subside and my friend, Kriss, gave me some advice.

"You need to put all this behind you. You should try internet dating. It's a good way to meet people, and so long as you only meet in the daytime and in a public place, it's safe enough. You just need to create a profile."

"I wouldn't know how to do that," I replied, hesitant. I made excuses. I wanted company, but I was afraid of hurting or being hurt again. Kriss was persistent, kept pushing and eventually set one up for me.

As soon as Kriss posted my profile online, the action started happening. We giggled like schoolgirls reading profiles and chat-up lines.

"Are you going to send a kiss back?" she asked me after one chat-up line. Now I was really scared. I was not ready. I was happy window shopping. Kriss answered the first couple of kisses on my behalf to show me what to do and how to vet the incoming responses. I got the hang of it.

The first date I went on was for a coffee. I was so nervous my smile developed a slight twitch. I arranged to meet at a local cafe so I could get there without getting lost in the fog of my injured brain. "Why on earth am I putting myself through all this?" I wondered.

I waited in the coffee shop as a tall, confident man strode towards me. He was dressed all in black and white with a cape and beret. He greeted me and I put out my hand, but he pulled me in for a hug. He took off his cape with a flourish and draped it on the chair. I looked for the closest exit and committed it to memory. I suspected that I might need it very soon. He sat and talked and talked and talked. Then he answered his phone and talked and talked and talked. I drank my coffee in silence, and then I ate a cake, also in silence. After the third phone call, he turned his attention to me and talked about himself again, explaining how important he was, and the calls were very important. I didn't make his "important" list because he proceeded to brag about being a Young Liberal – name-dropping his famous friends.

Eventually, I rose to leave and paid for half our bill.

"Can I see you again? I think we got along very well," he smiled.

"I don't think we have much in common, but thank you for meeting me," was my reply. I couldn't get out of there quickly enough. I shut the door of my car and drove home to the solitude and safety of my little house. Better no man than the wrong man.

"Dating is like buying a new coat," laughed Kriss. "You see one you like the look of and try it on. If it doesn't fit, you put it back on the rack and try another one."

There were a couple of short-term friendships but not relationships. Then I went out with one guy for a long time because he told me he was lonely, and I felt sorry for him. I really should not have tried to accommodate people to make them happy. I should have been looking for someone who wanted to make me happy, too. He added a couple of those heavy stones of negativity to my backpack. One was added when I found out he wanted to cheat on me and had made overtones towards my daughter, Jeanette. I broke up with him. He begged forgiveness, but the trust was gone. When you screw up a piece of paper, then try to smooth it out, it's never going to be the same.

All this took place on the eve of my 60th birthday. At first, I was shocked; then I was very sad and hurt. When I fully processed what had happened, I was angry, very angry. Angry at him for the disrespect he showed me and my darling Jeanette. Angry at his deception. Angry at myself for being taken in by such a master manipulator.

I had planned my birthday celebration by buying two tickets on the Puffing Billy Steam Train for a 'murder mystery ride and dinner.' I resolved to use those tickets, go forward and not look back. I wanted to wipe him out of my life because he didn't deserve to be in it.

"I'd love to go with you, Mum." It was Deb to the rescue.

"I'll take any opportunity to dress up and eat out," she said, and we laughed. So, on the night of my birthday, Deb and I dressed in 1920s clothes and boarded Puffing Billy to celebrate in style. I gazed at my elder daughter across the dining car table and realised how blessed I was. I was content in the knowledge that Deb would always, no matter what, have my back.

Over the next few weeks, I was lonely. I had moved to Altona and loved the holiday atmosphere of Pier Street and the history of The Homestead in the park by the beautiful pier. I was fairly close to the beach and went for long walks to feel the soothing salt sea air and absorb the calming seas.

I chose Altona to be closer to Jeanette and her two gorgeous girls, Emily and Samantha – not because of the memories of my milk bar experience but in spite of them. I just wanted to be on call to babysit, and I loved going to dinner or just doing a drop-in, as Jeanette called it.

Jeanette is a veterinary nurse, and I was delighted when she brought home eight tiny puppies to hand feed them when the mother couldn't look after her newborns. It was a big commitment. Those tiny bundles needed feeding every two hours, day and night.

When I heard about her tiny house guests, I did a drop-in. There was Jeanette, sitting on the floor, covered in tiny creatures with a cosy blanket in a cardboard box beside her. They still had their eyes closed as they crawled all over her. She painstakingly picked up each one, feeding it with a bottle, toileting it onto newspaper and cleaning it with a warm face washer before placing it in the box to have a full-bellied snooze. As I looked at Jeanette, my baby girl, and saw how accomplished and nurturing she was, I felt a gush of warm pride. I had raised two pretty wonderful women.

Apart from Jeanette and the girls, I didn't know many people in Altona, so I joined the historical society. I enjoyed learning about local history and giving tours to school kids who visited the homestead. I was working half-time as a Reading Recovery teacher, one-on-one and coping very well with that. Socially, I was filling my life with other things and not relying on a relationship to fulfil me, but I was still lonely.

My driving improved to the point where I could drive on familiar roads with more confidence. In the past, I had visited my friend from college, Jenny. I was honoured to be her witness when she married on a Lake Tyers farm. She loved nature and the countryside, but she eventually moved back to Phillip Island. Although I had been there many times in the past, my head injury meant I couldn't do that anymore, so Jenny drove the 2.5 hours to visit me.

Jenny and I have the same easy friendship that I have with Kriss. No matter how long it has been since I saw them, we ease straight back into our friendship, like putting on our favourite PJs. Comfortable and warm.

I have been blessed with a lot of great friends, but I wanted someone to sit on the couch with and watch TV.

At 60 years of age, I decided I didn't want another boyfriend, but I would like someone to have dinner with and go to the movies with occasionally. That would be perfect. On the dating site, I made a new profile that made it very clear what I was interested in doing. Almost immediately, I got a response from "David from Sunshine."

CHAPTER 27
David and Me

"Meet me at Mosaics in Pier Street Altona," David said. "I'm not much good on computers."

I drove to the cafe and parked outside. David was already there, watching me park and stifling a laugh. It made me even more nervous and I parked a bit too far from the kerb, but it would have to do.

David was shorter than he said, maybe an inch shorter than me. He was also a lot trimmer than his photo and very attractive. We sat at a table and started to suss each other out.

"Where does your family come from?" he asked.

"My mother was quite proud to be descended from the first white child born in Footscray. I am from pioneer Irish stock, and my dad, well, he was from a little place nobody has ever heard of – Crowlands, outside of Ararat," I said.

"My family comes from Crowlands," he chimed in. I didn't believe a word of it.

"Nobody's family comes from Crowlands," I thought. "There are only about four houses and a dog in Crowlands. He is obviously lying to impress me." Then I started to tell him a story about Crowlands in the pioneer days and David *finished the story*. I was stunned. His family did come from that small country town that held my father's heart and soul.

David had been married for 35 years to a wonderful woman whom he loved dearly. She had died from a brain tumour more than a year ago. He had nursed her until the end. He was grieving. David was lonely and tired of looking at four walls at home with his boxer dog, Odie. He wanted company, as I did.

After hearing his story, I thought, "This man needs a friend. I can be a good listener and friend to him," and we settled into a relaxed, easy conversation without any nerves or expectations.

We talked the afternoon away and the dinner crowd started to arrive, so we decided to leave.

"I'd like to see you again and take you out someplace really nice," David said.

I answered: "It doesn't have to be very nice. Just a pub is OK." I didn't want to go anywhere expensive because I planned on paying for myself. I liked him, but I didn't want him to pay and for me to feel indebted.

Our first date was to the Spottiswoode Hotel in Spotswood – the odd spelling of the hotel's name indicates its historical background, as that was the original name of the area. I had never been there before and the big open fire welcomed me in with a warm crackle. We took our seats and started the kind of more in-depth conversation, the kind that helps strangers connect and become friends. David was a good listener this time. When his meal came, it was something that he couldn't eat. I offered to swap, but he insisted he wasn't really hungry. He ate a little from his plate and then had the bread.

David closed his eyes and heaved a frustrated sigh.

"Oh no," he said. "You won't believe it. There's my best friend, his wife and a whole table of people I know here."

David acted a little annoyed. I wondered if he had inadvertently mentioned our date to his friend who came along for a stickybeak to check me out.

"Don't look over," he continued. "Maybe they won't notice us." A few minutes passed, and then a rather rotund woman in her 60s came over to the table gushing.

"Oh, isn't this lovely? So nice to see you've got someone!" David's deceased wife's friend, Anna, exclaimed. David excused himself and went to the toilet, leaving me with her.

"How long have you two been together? Where are you from? How did you meet?" I felt as if I was being interrogated, pumped for information that she could take back to the table to share with the gang in the other room. I wished David would come back and started to wonder if he had "done a runner" and left me to face the inquisition. Then she dropped a bombshell.

"So nice that he has found someone with his cancer and all," she smiled.

I sat quietly as Anna continued to talk about David's wife and David's cancer. David had not had a chance to tell me about his health issues, but the food issue made sense now. David returned to the table and tactfully got rid of our hovering voyeur. She scurried back to eager ears at her table.

"So ... where is your cancer?" I asked.

"Oh, bloody Anna," he said, "I wanted to tell you myself. I have carcinoid syndrome."

CHAPTER 28
David's Story

David had always loved sailing ships. He loved anything that floated. He was thrilled when his uncle got him a job at the Commonwealth Naval Dockyards at Williamstown.

Williamstown is next to his home suburb of Newport, south-west of Melbourne, on Port Phillip Bay.

The docks were steeped in history, and most of the people who worked there loved ships and sailing. Unfortunately, the environment proved toxic for David and many others.

When he worked there in the 1980s, one of the dockyards' main functions was to repair and refit naval ships in a drydock. The ships would be rusty and in need of repainting, so old paint would be removed by shot-blasting, which sent toxic dust cascading around the yard and into the workers' lunchroom. Then the ships were completely repainted with toxic paint from America.

David's work life was relatively uneventful, and he managed to avoid the violence for which the Painters and Dockers Union was famous.

He drove trucks and had to work with or dispose of dangerous chemicals and substances. The pipes on the naval ships were covered in asbestos as insulation.

"When ships were refitted, we had to cut it off with an angle grinder and tear it off with our bare hands," David recalled.

There were tons of toxic materials and matter loaded onto trucks and driven to tips, some of which were owned by the Australian Defence Force. Four tips were in Newport: a navy tip at the corner of Mason Street, one at Challis Street, another navy site at William Street and the Newport quarry on Johnston Street (now Newport Lakes). Other tips were at Ravenhall, in Deer Park, and another between Werribee and Little River. They also dumped chemicals at Kooringal Golf Course in Altona and on a massive Australian Defence Force-owned site behind the Sunshine tip in Hulett Street. This was later sold for housing.

Arsenic, asbestos, mercury, cadmium, organotin anti-fouling paints, oil from transformers and all the chemicals used in chrome plating and Parkerizing of parts – a trade name for a protective coating used on gun barrels. David and other drivers drove all those chemicals to a tip and unloaded them.

One fateful day, David and two other drivers loaded rusty old 44-gallon drums onto a truck and drove it from the dockyard to the Challis Street tip. The tip there had a giant pit with two underground oil tanks that had previously stored ship fuel. They leaked, so the navy repurposed them as navy waste dump pits.

While loading the truck, they noticed some drums were leaking mercury, which formed into small balls and rolled around the back of the truck. At the tip, the men rolled the drums to the edge of the 30-foot drop and into the pit. Boom! A huge yellow cloud of smoke rose from the tank and wafted over the men, the vehicles and the surrounding houses. Some of the drums had split open on impact, spewing out their toxic contents, which mixed with whatever else was already in the tanks.

An underground chemical fire ignited, billowing thick smoke that filled mouths, noses, throats, eyes and lungs. Coughing, the men used their hands to cover their noses and faces as they watched the horrific scene unfold.

The drums' contents mingled with chemicals and oil already in the pit, igniting the toxic concoction before fumes and chemicals were belching everywhere.

Quickly, David found a phone box to call the fire brigade. They arrived in breathing apparatus and sprayed on foam to douse the flames and control the fumes. It was too late for David and the others, who coughed as their chests and noses burned.

The after-effects were worse. Of the 24 men who drove chemicals from the naval dockyard trucks, breathing or swallowing the toxic substances they transported, 19 would prematurely die from cancer of the throat, oesophagus, lungs, stomach or bowel.

David told me: "I thought I was lucky to escape the Big C and relieved when I got recommended for a new post in a different part of the dockyard, glad to be away from the poison."

He went on to become a chauffeur for Commodore H.H. Dalrymple, and later when the docks were privatised, he drove for the general manager, Bill Millen.

When David was retrenched, he used his package to buy a house for himself, his wife Leanne and their three children.

His health suffered mildly at first. He stoically kept working until he realised his health problems were not resolving. He saw a doctor who seemed unconcerned by his random symptoms of "flushing and stomach pain." David carried on with life until he crumbled.

"A stabbing pain in the right side of my abdomen bent me in half and I was rushed into surgery at Williamstown Hospital with appendicitis," David recalled.

When the anaesthetic fog lifted, David was back on the ward.

"Mr King," the surgeon began. "We removed your appendix, but we found something else. You had a tumour near your appendix so we have removed that and sent it off to pathology."

Something was wrong. By the next day, the surgeon had stopped calling him Mr King and addressed him by his first name:

"David, unfortunately, the cancer is more widespread than we thought ... you have a very rare form of cancer called carcinoid syndrome, and this is very serious. Your life expectancy is around five years."

Alone in the hospital as he took the news, David could not focus on the surgeon's words after that.

His mind raced, but mostly he worried about life for Leanne and their fatherless children.

Anger boiled in him, just as the cancer had been allowed to percolate unchecked in him. He was angry at the dockyards for exposing him to the chemicals that were going to kill him, angry at himself for taking the job, angry at the doctor for not working a miracle and angry at God for letting this happen.

"I always had a belief in something greater than myself, but I would not say I was religious," David told me. "Leanne was not a believer, but she respected that I had beliefs and she bought me a gold cross and chain, which she put around my neck. I still wear it. I think that belief stopped me from sinking into despair. I had a glimmer of hope deep inside me and I clutched that tightly."

Chemotherapy followed and radiation ravaged his body. David shared with me the intimate details of his battle with cancer and the Black Dog:

"I was allergic to anti-nausea medication so I was doomed to suffer the full effects of the treatment without anything to combat that. To say I vomited a lot is an understatement. I went from a muscular 85 kilograms to 53 kilograms in a matter of weeks. I remember being curled up on the floor of the lounge room in front of the heater in the foetal position, sunk in depression and praying for relief. The weight of depression brings with it an isolated selfishness that is all-consuming."

Many people tried to reach out to him at that time, but his depression consumed him. His family suffered while he retreated inside himself to try to make sense of it all.

"It's a horrible feeling to be so sick and to never, ever be able to forget about it even for a minute," he said.

Then David said something that resonated with me.

"My illness seemed to define my whole self to others and I resented that," he said. "I wanted to scream, 'I am more than my cancer! Ask me about something else. Let's just have an ordinary conversation' because where does the conversation go after, 'I feel like crap, and I'm probably going to die?'"

I knew exactly what he meant. My experience was the same after my work accident. I hated that people looked at me and immediately saw my illness. I, too, wanted to scream: "I am more than my illness. I'm still me!"

Still, David had Leanne, who was a strong, tenacious person. She refused to give up. She launched into research mode and read everything she could find on carcinoid syndrome. She scoured the internet for any mention of treatment and was rewarded with an article that described an experimental treatment being trialled in Norway.

With a sliver of hope, Leanne sprang into action and phoned the doctor, who was conducting the research. She had a long talk with him, explaining David's situation.

Their hope was Sandostatin, a drug that a company was testing. Leanne wrote seeking more information and asking for suggestions on fighting carcinoid syndrome in Australia. A stack of hardcover books containing everything that was known about the syndrome and its possible treatments arrived from Norway. The package also contained extensive details about the trials being conducted. They took the information to Dr Ian Olver at Peter MacCallum Hospital on the corner of William and Little Lonsdale streets, Melbourne, and placed them on his desk. He was flabbergasted.

"How on earth did you get all this information?" the doctor asked, but Leanne's determined expression said it all.

"What followed was incredible," David said. "I am possibly the only person outside of Norway to be part of the trials. That drug saved my life and is now used to treat carcinoid tumours in Australia."

CHAPTER 29
Down But Not Out

David had difficulty breathing and soon discovered that his lungs were afflicted with pleural thickening, a disease that can be caused by asbestos exposure. Asbestos fibres cause tissue in the lungs to scar, which leads to thickening of the pleural lining. It is incurable but treatable.

David's dockyards' mates were all in agreement: "You should get yourself a lawyer."

Some other workers had gained compensation for the suffering they and their families endured as a result of asbestos exposure, so Leanne and David went to see a solicitor. They were told they had a good case and left it in the hands of the lawyers.

David waited for two years, and no compensation came. He contacted his member of parliament, Barry Jones, who got him a meeting with the relevant government department. David was assured that he had a good case and that it seemed the Commonwealth had a case to answer. He had been granted compensation for both carcinoid syndrome and the pleural thickening in his lungs, and the paperwork would be signed as soon as it was drawn up.

A few days later, the bottom fell out of his plans when the then prime minister Paul Keating called a general election. The government went into caretaker mode. All outstanding business and paperwork would not be signed until after the election. David and Leanne were in limbo. If only the election had been called a few days later they would have had their desperately needed compensation.

An election was held and the Labor government was replaced by the Howard Liberal government. Bronwyn Bishop was the new minister for the defence industry. A letter arrived from her saying they would not honour the commitment given by the previous government. His claim was denied.

David fought the system but to no avail.

The following is an excerpt from *That Disreputable Firm ... the inside story of Slater & Gordon* by Michael Cannon – Melbourne University Press 1998:
> David King consulted Slater & Gordon over a rare condition called Malignant Carcinoid of the Ileum – in layman's terms, cancer of the small intestine, which is the last section of intestine before it enters the colon. David, born in 1955, worked for the Defence Department at the Williamstown Naval Dockyards from 1982 to 1987. We have already seen the deadly results of the Commonwealth's failure to provide masks or

protective clothing for men stripping asbestos from ships being renovated at Williamstown. Even in the mid-1980s, nothing was yet being done to safeguard the Department's transport drivers like David King or inform them of any potential dangers. So, David and 27 other drivers simply loaded asbestos and other dangerous materials like powdered arsenic into open trucks, stamped down the loads to flatten them, and drove off to Sunshine and Werribee tips, trailing clouds of poisonous dust. During lunch breaks on the wharves, the drivers were also exposed to asbestos dust and chemicals drawn into the air-conditioning unit in their lunch room.

After 1986, David began experiencing palpitations, accelerated heartbeats, cramps and flushing of the face and neck. Severe abdominal pains began early in 1989. Two operations at Williamstown Hospital that year revealed David's intestinal cancer, which had already begun to spread through his lymphatic system. Despite a limited life expectancy, David attempted to take action against the Commonwealth through a Melbourne law firm. He was advised that his unusual disease was not compensable, either through the old Workers' Compensation Act or the Commonwealth Employees Compensation Act 1988. Nor, it appeared, could anything be done for the other comparatively young drivers once employed at the dockyards, of whom 13 had already died of various malignant tumours.

Settlement of the Arnold Simmons case in 1991 gave new hope to David King. He went to Slater & Gordon, who issued a negligence writ in the County Court, and called for new medical reports. The matter dragged on for a considerable time as researchers combed the world scientific literature in search of similar cases. Finally, they reported that they could find little direct evidence to connect David's rare type of cancer to asbestos exposure. An appeal to Comcare Australia in 1994 to do something for the sick man was rejected on similar grounds.

In September, 1996, the Commonwealth decided to compromise the five-year-old County Court action before it became a public hearing. Then a five-figure sum was offered to include all legal costs and disbursements without any admission of liability. In satisfaction for all past and future claims, (re asbestos exposure) there seemed no alternative but to accept the offer.

The public servants involved had learnt a lot about protecting their own backs. In letting go of a modest amount of taxpayers' money, they forced the plaintiff to agree to keep confidential the terms of the settlement and not disclose same to the media. I find this disgusting, and wonder if they ever gave thought to the public interest, or to 40-year-old David King taking daily doses of morphine to relieve his desperate agony.

The compensation was eaten up by legal costs, and that left very little after the settlement.

David had tried everything to get compensation.

We had both been screwed over by the system.

David's story touched my heart. I immediately drew parallels between his battle with illness and my head injury. Both incidents had radically turned our lives upside down and we were both still struggling to accommodate our illnesses in our daily lives. We had both sought legal action and some type of justice from our employers. Both of us had been trampled over by the legal system. David and I shared a bond because of the first-hand knowledge of struggling to negotiate the minefield of WorkCover procedures and court hearings, only to be let down by the process and screwed over by expenses related to bringing a court action against the church or the government.

We bonded over the huge impacts our work accidents had on our daily lives. We were both struggling to start a new life and faced an uncertain future.

CHAPTER 30
To Boldly Go ...

Our second date took me back to my hometown of Yarraville and to The Sun Theatre, which I loved. After the movie, we walked to the Railway Hotel for a meal. We talked some more and got to know each other.

This conversation filled in a lot of gaps in our stories. We were more candid with each other and eased into a comfortable friendship.

David had had a terrible childhood – the opposite of mine. As we got to know each other, we found we had more in common than we thought possible. Many times our paths had crossed as we weaved in and out of each other's lives.

David was one of the boys who hung around our milk bar in Altona. He was one of those bikies at the kindergarten working bee all those years ago. He remembered me from that day when I had given him an iced drink while he shovelled tanbark under the playground equipment.

A prowler had stolen his sister's underwear from her home in Newport before invading her home. David found the culprit, caught him in the act and made him regret ever starting his perverted hobby.

When we both had young families, we had lived a few houses apart in Talintyre Road, West Sunshine, but we had never met. He remembered seeing Deborah in her North Melbourne footy jumper as she walked past his house towards the shops.

We had attended the same rock concerts and enjoyed the same kind of music. We already knew we had Crowlands connections, but the pièce de résistance was the discovery that our two families had married into each other so we were distantly related.

Jeanette and Deborah supported me through the hell of being injured and through the long rehab and healing process to get me as far as I could go. I will never be the same as I was, but I have come to terms with who I am now. It's no good grieving for the person I was – she has gone. I'm not her, but I'm a pretty good facsimile.

I wanted to do something for them to express my love and thanks for their unending support. A trip to America had been planned long before I met David, so I asked my daughters if they would mind if David joined us on the second leg of the journey. They agreed this would be a good way for them to get to know him.

We set off on our American adventure. Jeanette and her girls, Emily and Samantha, had spent five days with me, going to Disneyland every day before we met up with Deb and her boys, Conor and Dan, in New York.

David met us at the Los Angeles International Airport, dishevelled and sweaty. He had travelled from Australia in a plane with faulty air-conditioning and no entertainment, so it had been a torturous flight.

On arrival, American security pulled David aside, a single man travelling alone. He had triggered their radars because he had visited most of the world, including the Middle East. After a gruelling hour of questioning, enormous soldiers with guns checked his story that he had been in the military and let him go to meet us.

New York was amazing. Deb and the boys greeted their nana with big hugs and we all explored Central Park, the zoo, the museums, the art galleries, the shops and Grand Central Station – an instantly recognisable set from so many of my favourite movies. We even saw *The Lion King* on Broadway.

Grand Central Station is such a beautiful building and I was in awe remembering the well-known scenes from movies that had been filmed there. As I took in the intricacies of the imposing staircase, I heard Conor's voice ring out: "There's Grandad."

Sure enough, there was my ex-husband, Fred, with his wife, exploring the same location at the exact same time. I introduced him to David, and we

Making new memories in Central Park, New York. From left: Conor, Dan, David, me, Samantha, Jeanette and Emily. Deb behind the camera.

had a chat before going on our way. We had all found ourselves in the one spot in America, halfway around the world from our homes in Australia. What are the odds of that happening? Coincidence is an amazing thing.

In the hustle and bustle of Times Square, 12-year-old Emily was fascinated by the Naked Cowboy – a busker who entertained crowds, his Tighty Whities underwear concealed only by his guitar. She approached him nervously and stuffed a crumpled dollar note into the hole in his guitar before giggling with hunched shoulders and scurrying back to us.

My girls got to know David very well on that trip and gave me the thumbs up. They approved.

We all went back to California and Disneyland because five days were not enough for Emily and Samantha, while Conor and Dan had yet to discover the joys of the "happiest kingdom of them all."

I will forever remember the look on my grandchildren's little faces on those magical rides and at the grand parade. I was thrilled to go on the Star Wars ride with grandsons Conor and Dan. They have inherited my love of movies and we always discuss the latest flicks on TV or the cinema. They are growing into delightful, kind, interesting young men now, and my heart swells with pride when I see them.

My granddaughters, Emily and Samantha, were little when we went on the America trip and both have grown into compassionate, beautiful souls that shine through their stunning faces. I like them. I don't just love my grandchildren; I really like the people they have become. David loves and is loved by my family too, which warms my heart.

One day, my whole extended family were so pleased to see me happy that they welcomed David with open arms, literally. My brother, Gerald, threw his arms around David and hugged him, giving him the sort of welcome our wonderful dad would have provided if only he had been able to meet him.

David and I remained friends for a long time before either of us was ready to commit. As soon as our friendship turned into a romantic relationship, David wanted to get married. I was gun-shy after my bad experiences of committed relationships. I clung to my independence, even though I could not imagine life without David.

David asked me to marry him three times. The first two times I said, "Ask me next year." Then, one day in 2013, we were sitting watching TV on my villa unit couch in Wren Street, Altona.

"Look," David said. "I think we should get married. I know they say it's the same if we live together, but it's not the same for me. I want to be married to you, forever."

I replied, "Alright then," and three months later, we walked down the aisle at St Carthage's Church, Parkville, to the music of The Beatles, chosen by David:

In My Life

"There are places I'll remember
All my life, though some have changed
Some forever, not for better
Some have gone and some remain

All these places have their moments
With lovers and friends, I still can recall

Some are dead and some are living
In my life, I've loved them all

But of all these friends and lovers
There is no one compares with you
And these memories lose their meaning
When I think of love as something new

Though I know I'll never lose affection
For people and things that went before
I know I'll often stop and think about them
In my life, I love you more

Though I know I'll never lose affection
For people and things that went before
I know I'll often stop and think about them
In my life, I love you more

In my life, I love you more."
(Paul McCartney and John Lennon)

David and I, in love and married at last. Photo: Mark Phillips.

Deb gave David the best endorsement she could give anyone when she took me aside. "You know you married a younger version of your father, don't you?"

That was the start of our new adventures. We decided to enjoy every moment we shared and not waste the time we had together. We went to Venice, England and Malta and cruised the Mediterranean Greek islands on our honeymoon.

David's health was up and down. We decided to live life to the fullest while we could and when his health allowed. We cruised to New Zealand, the Caribbean and Hawaii and drove through more of the USA on a bus tour of national parks.

We couldn't get full insurance coverage and took a big risk travelling overseas. If he got sick while we were travelling, the cost of medical assistance would be astronomical. The quality of treatment could not be relied upon. We could not be sure other doctors would be familiar with David's rare form of cancer. Nevertheless, after our European adventures, we took our faith, hope and courage into our hands and embarked on many more journeys together.

We explored the USA together three times.

There were lots of shared adventures before and after we married.

David's family includes me in their celebrations, and I love to play with his grandchildren and enjoy watching them grow and change into unique little people that I love.

David looks after me as much as I look after him. He knows when to hold my hand to help me regain my balance. He knows when I have had enough socialising and need to leave. He takes care of the tasks that my head doesn't let me do. He turns his music down when my sensory overload kicks in.

For my part, I look after David when his cancer causes him to relapse or when his nerve pain is so bad nothing will take the edge off except a massage from me with Voltarin cream.

I make sure he looks after his diet and his diabetes. When I find myself asking "Have you checked your sugar?" for the umpteenth time that day, I search his face for a sign he might be sick of my prompting, but it's never there.

He and I complement each other – two sides of the same coin. He excels at all the things that I fail miserably at and vice versa.

We found each other late in life and married when we were in our sixties, but I feel blessed to have found him, and he feels the same. We are like teenagers in each other's company. I missed out on my actual teenage years, but I am making up for that now. We hold hands when we go for a walk or when we sit watching TV. David tells me every day that he loves me, and I tell him the same.

There have been times when I thought I would lose him to his dreaded carcinoid syndrome and had to call ambulances to revive him. I have sat with him in emergency departments on countless occasions. Whenever that happens, I can rely on Jeanette and Deb to support us both through whatever comes.

We don't know what the future holds. We do know we can face it together, sharing the good times and the bad.

We travel life's journey together, in the company of those we have met along the way. We carry an assortment of rocks and feathers on our backs as we help each other and share the load.

Thank you for being part of my journey. My hope is that I will be a warming feather in your backpack.

MY 'FEATHER' FRIENDS

My friends who make my life and backpack lighter.

Karl and Maria remain constant feathers on my journey.

Jill, Clara and me at a birthday celebration.

Dana and me as Jack Sparrow, arrrgh.

www.ingramcontent.com/pod-product-compliance
Lightning Source LLC
Chambersburg PA
CBRC091957300426
44109CB00007BA/158

Buffy bought us together and we remain great friends. Lucy (left) and Dana with me on my wedding day.

Jeff and Joan when they were newly weds.

Joe and Kriss. Kriss gave me some timely advice when I needed it and helped me onto the modern dating scene. She has been a enduring friend.